REAGAN'S ROOTS

The People and Places
That Shaped His Character

PETER HANNAFORD

Library of Congress Cataloging-in-Publication Data

Hannaford, Peter.

Reagan's roots : the people and placers that shaped his character / Peter Hannaford.

   p. cm.

ISBN 978-1-884592-57-7

1. Reagan, Ronald—Childhood and youth. 2. Presidents—United States—Biography. I. Title.

E877.2.H349 2012

973.927092—dc23

[B]

                    2011040326

ISBN 9781884592577

Copyright ©2012 Peter Hannaford

First edition, First printing

Published by Images from the Past, Inc.
www.imagesfromthepast.com
PO Box 137, Bennington VT 05201
Tordis Ilg Isselhardt, Publisher

Printed in the USA

Design and Production: Ron Toelke Associates, Chatham, NY

Printer: Versa Press, Inc., East Peoria, IL

REAGAN'S ROOTS

The People and Places
That Shaped His Character

PETER HANNAFORD

IMAGES FROM THE PAST
Bennington, VT

Books by Peter Hannaford

Reagan's Roots

Presidential Retreats

Ronald Reagan and His Ranch:
The Western White House, 1981–89

The Quotable Calvin Coolidge

The Essential George Washington

The Quotable Ronald Reagan

My Heart Goes Home: A Hudson Valley Memoir (editor)

Recollections of Reagan

Remembering Reagan (co-author)

Talking Back to the Media

The Reagans: A Political Portrait

Dedicated to the memory of

Nelle and Jack Reagan,

who gave us one of our best presidents

Contents

Acknowledgments

My special thanks go to Dr. J. David Arnold, president of Eureka College, and his colleagues for readily opening archives and files and answering many questions having to do with Ronald Reagan's college days and his strong continuing ties with the college in the years following his graduation. Especially helpful were Anthony Glass, director of the Melick Library and archivist of the college; Mike Murtagh, vice president of development and alumni relations; John D. Morris, director of development of the Ronald W. Reagan Leadership Program; Dr. Brian Sajko, curator of the Reagan Museum; and Jyl Krause, executive assistant to the president.

Thanks also go to Ann Lewis, chairman of Dixon's Reagan Centennial Commission and vice chairman of the State of Illinois Reagan Centennial Commission, who provided invaluable introductions to the people and places in Dixon that brought Dutch Reagan's days in that city to life. She and her husband, Dr. Don Lewis, also welcomed me with their Dixon hospitality.

Others who were helpful include Richard Bednar, who provided the televised interview of then-President Reagan discussing the importance of coach Ralph McKinzie in his life; Joan Johnson, of the Reagan Birthplace and Museum in Tampico; Connie Lange, executive director of the Ronald Reagan Boyhood Home in Dixon; Denise McLouglin, family history coordinator of the Tampico Area

Historical Society; Eureka College professor Junius Rodriguez; Lynn Roe, director of the Dixon Public Library; and Fran Swarbrick of the Loveland Museum, Dixon.

I also thank my wife, Irene, for her warm encouragement and for spotting typos in the manuscript, and publisher Tordis Isselhardt, editor Glenn Novak, and designer Ron Toelke for making the ultimate book possible.

One spring day in 2010 I was in Charlottesville, Virginia, to give a talk at the Miller Center of Public Affairs at the University of Virginia. The topic was President Reagan's strategy for bringing the Cold War to a successful conclusion. That strategy was a long time in development (its antecedents predated his presidency) and was carried out with energy, imagination, and great determination. When I finished my remarks, the program host asked the audience for questions. I expected these to be about details of the Cold War strategy.

To my surprise, a man stood and asked this question: "Can you tell us the source or sources of Ronald Reagan's character?"

I thought for a moment, then said, "Yes. In a word, 'Illinois.'"

All the years of my knowing, working for, and studying Ronald Reagan suddenly crystallized with that man's question.

The characteristics we most often associate with Reagan—self-confidence, self-reliance, optimism, modesty, loyalty, tolerance, good humor, determination, and reverence for God—all came from his forebears, his parents, teachers, coaches, clergy, and boyhood friends. And they were all in Illinois. More particularly, they were in the northwestern quarter of Illinois.

If you look at a map of Illinois and divide it into the four quarters of the compass, you will find that virtually all the years of Ronald Reagan's childhood, youth, and initial adulthood occurred within that one northwestern area, in a series of towns and small cities such as Tampico, Monmouth, Galesburg, Dixon, and Eureka. This is rural America, a land of rich, deep soil, mostly given to farming, but also to some manufacturing. A strong work ethic prevailed and prevails throughout the area.

I explained to my questioner and the audience that by the time Ronald Reagan got his first job out of college just across the Mississippi River in Davenport, Iowa, he was twenty-one and his character (but not his political philosophy) was fully formed.

His forebears were Irish and Scottish and English, typical of the settlers of northwestern Illinois in the mid-nineteenth century. Most of them had been tenant farmers looking for a new life across the sea, in which they could own some land, have a home of their own, and make a decent life for their families.

These forebears are long gone; however, the people directly in Ronald's Reagan life who contributed to the development of his character you will meet in these pages. You will also see the places where they lived and worked and where he lived. Some of these towns are a little bigger today, some about same now as then, and some a little smaller, but if you were to spend some time visiting them, it would not be hard to imagine that the pace of life today in these places is not a great deal different from what it was when Ronald Reagan was young.

Peter Hannaford

Eureka, California

August 2011

Chapter One

Old Country,
New World

The Reagans

Thomas and Margaret O'Regan and their six children lived in a
stone hut with a dirt floor in a collection of such huts called Doolis in
Ireland's County Tipperary. It was close by the town of Ballyporeen.
Their brood consisted of three girls and three boys. The youngest
boy was Michael, born in 1829.

Tom, like his neighbors, was a tenant farmer, working for an
absentee landlord, a Member of Parliament. His sons, as soon as they
were old enough, were expected to help him in the fields.

Like thousands of others, they grew potatoes on a small patch of
land. The potato was the staple of their diet.

3

Laws from the seventeenth and eighteenth centuries prohibited Irish Catholics from owning or leasing land, from voting or holding office, from entering a profession or obtaining an education. Most of these had been repealed or reformed by 1829, the year Michael was born, but the traditions tended to remain.

One earlier law, the "Middleman Law," allowed absentee landlords to hire agents or middlemen to manage their lands. The income of these agents depended upon how many plots of land they managed and from which they could extract rents. This was an incentive to divide and redivide small plots to make more of them. The plots were so small that, as a practical matter, the only crop that could be cultivated was the potato. Most of the crop was shipped to England to satisfy a growing demand for the tuber. Each tenant was permitted to keep a small amount of what he produced in order to feed his family.

There was neither the time nor the inclination to educate children. They would be needed in the fields.

There had been other diseases to hit potato crops, but in 1844 a new one, *Phytophthora infestans*—soon known as the blight—arrived in many parts of Europe. It has since been theorized that it came in shipments of Peruvian guano, widely used at the time in the British Isles as fertilizer. Another theory was that it came in American clipper ships carrying American-grown potatoes. Whatever the cause, it was devastating for several years.

The government in London organized committees and commissions to make recommendations but did little to alleviate the problem. In Ireland, where life for tenant farmer families had always been hard, the blight brought death by starvation to approximately one million people between 1845 and 1850.

The O'Reagans' Dilemma

Tom and Margaret O'Reagan talked about emigrating to the New World, but nothing came of it, because they could not afford the passage for themselves and six offspring, and Margaret and the three girls were already weak from undernourishment.

Young Michael was a bright boy. A teacher in Ballyporeen saw potential in him and quietly taught him to read. This fueled his ambition to go into the larger world and make something of himself.

In 1852, at the age of twenty-three, he left County Tipperary for London, taking with him a pretty girl a year younger, Catherine Mulcahy. They were married in a Catholic church on October 30 that year. In the register the priest wrote Michael's surname with the Irish spelling, "Regan," but Michael signed it English-style, "Reagan." Catherine was illiterate and so could only place a mark where her signature would go.

Their first child, Thomas, was born the following spring, May 15, 1853. John Michael (later to become Jack Reagan's father) came a year later, on May 23, 1854. Margaret was born November 3, 1855.

Michael found work in a soap factory. Saving enough money to emigrate to North America was a clear and persistent objective. He had stayed in touch with his older brothers, Nicholas and John, and began to make plans. By 1856 he had apparently saved enough money to take his wife and children to America. Presumably, his brothers had saved enough for their own passage, for they joined him and his family for the voyage.

Conditions on such ships were usually very bad. The ships were crowded, and sanitation was minimal. Michael may well have learned about this in advance and, in saving for the trip, put some money aside to take food aboard and perhaps obtain slightly better than normal accommodations for the journey. In any case, they all survived the trip.

Their initial destination was Canada, which makes it likely they sailed from Liverpool, for that was the main port where lumber-laden Canadian ships unloaded their cargo. Since these ships would otherwise return home empty, hauling emigrants became a lucrative business. (Between 1845 and 1852 nearly one million Irish emigrated, causing the island's population to drop by approximately 25 percent.)

Bound for Illinois

Although there is not a surviving record, it is likely that Michael and his family and brothers landed in Halifax, Nova Scotia, perhaps in 1856. They stayed for a few weeks, likely scouting out the best way to continue their journey westward, since they were headed for the United States.

What little Michael knew about the United States was that it was a land of great opportunity. His goal was to own land that he could make productive. From Halifax or some other port, the family made its way westward to the Great Lakes, likely by a combination of ship, rail, and canal boat. Probably they passed through Chicago, from where they headed due west across Illinois to Fair Haven, where they stopped.

With his brothers Nicholas and John, Michael built a small house in Fair Haven. He also cleared, cultivated, and planted sixteen acres, probably in corn. Michael and Catherine had a fourth child, William, born in 1859.

By 1860, Michael had realized his ownership dream. In the census that year he was listed as "a farmer" who owned real estate with a value of $1,120 and "personal property" worth $150.

Michael's son John helped work the family land as a young man. Then, in 1873, when he was nineteen, he moved to Fulton, about twenty miles away, to work at a grain elevator. Four years later, he claimed two parcels under the Homestead Act back near his family's farm. These were Sections 21 and 22. His uncle Nicholas had a claim on Section 23. There were many small black oaks on John's property, and he cleared them by himself, then planted corn and garden vegetables. His brothers and uncles helped him build a two-room house.

In 1878, the year after he had staked his claim, John married Jenny Cusick. She was frail and unable to help with much of the work on the new farm. She was, however, able to bear three children: Catherine, born in 1879; William, born in 1881; and John Edward ("Jack"), born in 1883.

Jack, who was to become Ronald Reagan's father, had only happy memories of times with his parents. There were visits with Great Uncle Nicholas and his wife, Maria, and with Uncle Bill and his large family. Even as a small boy, Jack had "jobs" on the farm, such as chasing away crows, lest they dig up the recently planted corn seed.

This idyll ended abruptly for Jack in 1889 when both his parents died of tuberculosis within a week of each other. Jack's sister and brother went to live with their uncle Bill. Jack was too young to do heavy farm chores, so he was sent to live with his aunt Margaret and her husband, Orson Baldwin. They lived in the village of Bennett, Iowa, where Baldwin owned a general store. Margaret was a milliner and made occasional buying trips to Chicago to offer local women a selection of stylish new hats.

Margaret had been thirty-eight when she married Baldwin, a bachelor of fifty-nine, so their firsthand knowledge of small boys was nearly nonexistent. She was a devout Catholic and a disciplinarian; he was a closed-mouth man wrapped up in his business.

The town of Bennett had been founded only in 1884 as a railroad depot site between Cedar Rapids and Clinton, Iowa. Baldwin thought the town had great promise and moved Margaret and himself there from Davenport to open the store. Life was more difficult than he had expected, for he had two competitors in the small town.

Before long young Jack gained a reputation as a prankster. Margaret, having no real understanding of children's behavior, did not realize that the pranks were an unconscious bid by Jack for love and attention, something he had received little of since the death of his parents.

He had difficulty with his school subjects and thus did not like school. He dropped out after completing the sixth grade. He was twelve and went to work in the store. In his spare time he threw himself into sports, which he loved. He saved his pennies to attend the frequent wrestling matches that came to town. He also joined a boys' baseball team.

At age sixteen (in 1899) he moved back to Fulton, about thirty miles east of Bennett. He moved into the home of his grandmother Catherine, now sixty-six. His brother William also lived in Fulton, working at the same grain elevator where their father, John, had worked.

Their sister Kate worked in the millinery department of a local dry goods store and helped him get a job there. He found he liked selling shoes, and it soon became his specialty. He liked children and admired the pretty young women who came to try on shoes.

He talked often of going west as a latter-day pioneer, just as his grandfather Michael had done in coming to the New World, but nothing came of it. He stayed at the J. D. Broadhead Dry Goods Store for eight years. He was a good shoe salesman, and his dark good looks and charming manner made him attractive to many of the town's young women. Alas, he had also developed a fondness for drink, which became well known and caused many parents to declare him off limits to their daughters.

This did not deter Nelle Clyde Wilson.

The Wilsons

In 1835 John Wilson had joined his elder brother, William Ronald, and his wife, Susan Napier Wilson, on their voyage to the New World. They had lived in Renfrewshire, Scotland. It was said that Susan had been disowned by her family. The trio landed in Halifax and soon headed west for Ontario, where the two men joined a rebel group fighting for control of the government of Upper Canada. In 1837 they joined the effort of firebrand reformer William Lyon Mackenzie to take over Toronto. This failed, and the Wilson brothers and Susan made their way to the United States.

In September 1839 the trio arrived in Dent's Grove, in Illinois' Clyde Township (Whiteside County). Susan died soon afterward. John later wrote an account in the Wilson family Bible of his sister-in-law's grief over her estrangement from her own family in Scotland, the Napiers.

Two years later, on November 28, 1841, John Wilson married Jane Blue. She was the daughter of Donald and Catharine MacFairlain Blue of the Scottish Highlands. Donald Blue had been a fellow member of Mackenzie's rebels in the insurgency in Ontario.

The Wilson brothers and Blue had staked land claims at Dent's Grove. This was an unpopular action with established local farmers. The newcomers, however, declared their intention to stay (implying they were willing to fight to do so), and the county committee decided not to oppose them.

John's bachelor brother, William, left for California and the promise of gold in 1852. John and Jane's son Thomas was born that year. Soon after, John, along with his father-in-law, Donald Blue, succumbed to the gold lure and left for California themselves. They returned, empty-handed, in 1855.

Ultimately, John and Jane had eight children who survived to adulthood. Thomas, however, was particularly favored by Jane. She had survived the grief of learning that two of her brothers had died of starvation on Pike's Peak on a fruitless quest for gold. Along with that, she had been forced to manage the family herself while husband John was off in the California goldfields for three years.

She found solace in her deep Protestant faith, but the other experiences had left her with a very serious and reserved nature. Ultimately with a brood of eight children, Jane, as matriarch, saw to it that her family attended church every Sunday, which included two long sermons interspersed with prayers, hymns, and readings. The Bible was a dominant factor in the family's daily life.

In 1879 son Thomas married Mary Anne Elsey, who had been born in Epsom, Surrey, England, on December 27, 1843. Her parents were Robert and Mary Baker Elsey. They, along with five children and an orphaned nephew, Henry Elsey, had emigrated to New York in 1849. The following year Robert Elsey had died. Mrs. Elsey found enough work to get them to Elgin, Illinois, in 1851, where people she knew lived. In 1852 she married H. C. Wesley. In time they moved to Clyde Township in Whiteside County.[1]

On July 24, 1883, Nelle Clyde Wilson was born, the young-est of seven children of Thomas and Mary Anne Elsey Wilson. Unaccountably, in 1890 Thomas left the family and was not heard from for several years. Finally, when his mother, Jane, was on her deathbed in 1894, one of Thomas's brothers found him in Chicago and persuaded him to return home. Jane's obituary states that "there was one deep-seated yearning in the mother's heart to see once more for the last time the one son, Thomas, gone so long, and the son came and mother and son looked into each other's eyes and she was satisfied."

Nelle and Jack

Nelle's father, Thomas, now back home for good, shared the opinion of many Clyde Township mothers that Jack Reagan, with his fond-ness for liquor, was unsuitable as a mate for his daughter. Nevertheless, Jack was charming and handsome, and Nelle and he took a shine to each other. Nelle was petite and pretty, with auburn hair, blue eyes, and a vivacious personality.

Nelle's mother died on October 6, 1900, at age fifty-six. She had been deeply committed to her Protestant church—a commitment that would be passed down to her daughter. She had a favorite poem that described her philosophy and which she imparted to Nelle:

I live for those who love me, for those who know me true,

For the Heaven that smiles above me, and awaits my spirit, too,

For the human ties that bind me, for the task by God

assigned me,

For the bright hopes left behind me, and the Good that

I can do.

Guided by that, she always looked for the good in people and strived to help all who needed help.

After courting for several years, Nelle and Jack were married on November 8, 1904, in Fulton, where Jack lived, in the rectory of Immaculate Conception, the Catholic church he attended from time to time. Nelle's brother Alex gave the bride away.

They lived in Fulton because Jack's job was there. Nelle became used to Jack's weekend "benders," which he took with his brother William. She did not hold this against him, excusing it as something Irishmen do out of habit. Jack was friendly when he drank, but his brother turned surly. Indeed, at one point William spent several months in the county jail for "drunk and disorderly conduct." When he was sober, William ran a cigar store.

Nelle saw in Jack an ambition to have people respect him. He wanted to succeed well enough at business to provide a decent life for Nelle and himself, but he did not have a money drive. Instead, it was a drive for self-worth. Nelle did not see him getting that in Fulton or at the Broadhead store where he worked. She also saw William as a negative influence on her husband.

She persuaded Jack to apply for a job at the H. C. Pitney dry goods store in Tampico, twenty-six miles from Fulton. He got the job, and they moved in February 1906.

Chapter Two

Tampico

Today, Tampico's short Main Street is not as densely filled with buildings as it was when Jack and Nelle Reagan arrived in town in 1906, but those that remain are typical of rural Illinois small-town architecture of the 1870s. In 1872, '74, and '76 the town was visited by fires, and in 1874 by a tornado as well. The latter destroyed approximately forty buildings. With each calamity, many buildings had to be rebuilt or replaced.

Tampico (pronounced TAMP-IKKO) was built in a marshy area (drained in 1863–64). It saw its first white settlers in 1852 and became a township in 1861. In 1871 the Chicago, Burlington and Quincy Railroad built a line through Tampico, and a small boom resulted. The town was incorporated in 1875. In 1899 construction began on the Hennepin Canal, one mile east of Tampico.

In the 1910 census, Tampico was recorded as having 1,276 residents (the 2010 census counted 790, up 18 from that of 2000). Tampico served mostly as a market town for nearby farms. The railroad supplied goods from distant cities and hauled out grain (there were two grain elevators). Most people living in the town were in businesses serving the farming hinterland. Few had more than a grade-school education. No one was rich, but then no one starved, either. Not many had traveled as far as Chicago. Trips to Dixon or Fulton, each about twenty-five miles away, were big events for Tampicans.

The Main Street consisted of two-story buildings abutting each other, with stores on the ground floor and apartments above. Jack and Nelle found a six-room apartment at 111 Main Street above a bakery. Across the street in adjoining storefronts was the H. C. Pitney store, where Jack had been hired as a salesman.

The apartment was comfortable enough by the standards of the day for a young couple planning to have a family. The building had been built in 1895 by Fred Seymour, who also built the adjoining one, using a common wall and leaving three windows in the wall so the two apartments could connect. He put his grocery store in the ground-floor space of the second building. Nelle and Mrs. Seymour became good friends.

The Reagans' apartment had three bedrooms, a parlor, a dining room, and a kitchen. It also had a back porch, which they—

usually Nelle—used often to go outside to the pump to get water, because the apartment had no running water. Also, there was an outhouse out back, as there was no bathroom in the apartment. Bathing was done in a portable tub in the kitchen, using water hauled up the stairs and heated on one of their three coal stoves. Jack rarely helped Nelle to haul water or coal up the steep stairs. Despite these shortcomings and the work that it entailed for her, she did not complain. After all, they did have electricity, the stoves, and a party-line telephone.

Settling In

Jack was soon popular with the Pitney store's customers. Women, especially, were taken by his attention and warm manner. Myrtle Denison, a young woman during those days in Tampico, was quoted many years later as saying, "I bought my first pair of button shoes from there. I thought Jack was the most terrific thing ever."[1]

Nelle began attending the Christian Church (Disciples of Christ), a denomination derived from Presbyterianism. Her Bible was a constant companion.

She and Jack talked of starting a family. On September 16, 1908, John Neil Reagan was born in the apartment. He was called Neil (and a few years later acquired the nickname "Moon"). Not long after, Father Defore from the Catholic church called on the Reagans. According to Neil, his mother said the priest told her it was time to baptize her son. She said she wasn't sure. Father Defore is reported to have then said, "You don't have any choice, Nellie. You promised to bring up the children as Catholic when you were married to Jack in Fulton." She said she had been told nothing about that, so Father Defore asked Jack to explain why that was the case. Jack said that the priest who married them said he would talk to her about it but forgot to and that he, Jack, had forgotten all about it until this meeting.[2]

The result of this discussion was that Neil was baptized a Catholic. Nelle and Jack also made an agreement that their children would be raised as Catholic, but as soon as they were old enough to make their own decisions they were free to choose their religion.

On Easter Sunday, March 27, 1910, Nelle became a member of the Disciples of Christ. A few weeks later she was pregnant again. On Sunday night, February 5, 1911, an unusually heavy snowstorm hit Tampico. By the time it was spent it had dumped ten inches of snow on the area. Most roads were impassable. In the early hours of Monday morning, Nelle went into labor. She was having difficulty. Jack sent young Neil, not quite three, to be with neighbors, then worked his way to Dr. H. A. Terry's house, only to find that the doctor was already out on a call. He then made his way to the home of Mrs. Roy Rasine, a midwife, who accompanied him back to the apartment to help Nelle, who was in the front bedroom. The doctor arrived soon after. The baby was slow in coming.

Finally, the plump ten-pound boy came, squealing loudly. Jack looked him over closely and said, "For such a little bit of a Dutchman, he sure makes a hell of a noise, doesn't he?" Nelle said faintly, "I think he's perfectly wonderful."

Jack had inadvertently given his second son a nickname, "Dutch," that would stay with him until he left the Midwest for Hollywood in 1937. Nelle was very happy to have two sons to raise. Jack, meanwhile, had been told by the doctor that Nelle would not be able to have any more children.

Two Lively Boys

When Ronald was about four months old, the family moved from above the bakery to a single-family house a block south, at 104 Glassburn Street, across from Railroad Park (in recent years renamed Reagan Park). They lived there for nearly four years.

As soon as Ronald was old enough to walk, Nelle would take them to the park to watch the trains and play around the old Civil War cannon and its companion pyramid of cannonballs. One day, when Nelle was distracted, five-year-old Neil, with Ronald toddling after him, made his way across the park. Together, they crawled between the cars of a stopped freight train to get some ice chips from an ice wagon parked there. They crawled back between the cars just moments before the train let out a cloud of steam and a loud whistle and began to pull out of the station. Nelle, seeing this, was horrified, but the boys were safe. Ron later recalled that she "earlifted" them home to receive "proper punishment."

When he was three, Ron rode a small homemade car in Tampico's annual summer Homecoming Parade—with the Stars and Stripes flapping from its front.

Nelle joined a drama group that met above the bank in what was called "the Opera House." Although neither parent was demonstrative with hugs and kisses (nor did the boys get many), Jack did like to please Nelle, so he agreed to appear with her in an occasional play.

Nelle's Mission

Nelle's church activity increased. She took the children with her to prayer meetings every Wednesday and Sunday night. On Sunday mornings, the boys attended Sunday school. While Jack occasionally attended the Catholic church and joined the Knights of Columbus, he was not a regular churchgoer. Nelle began to write the church's notices for the local paper and recite poetry to church groups.

Nelle had promised her mother, Mary, on Mary's deathbed that she would always care for the poor and the helpless—anyone in need of succor. She soon made it her personal ministry to regularly visit patients in the local hospital, a mental institution, a tuberculosis sanatorium, and the county jail. She took not only her Bible, but also apples and cookies to the inmates in the jail.

To Chicago

Early in 1915, Pitney sold his store, which resulted in Jack's having to find another job. He applied for one at the big Fair Department

Store in Chicago and was accepted. This involved the longest-distance move of their lives for both Jack and Nelle. (They would return to Tampico, but they did not know this at the time.)

They rented a flat that had no hot water on the South Side of Chicago (832 East Fifty-seventh Street), near the University of Chicago campus and not far from the Fair store on South State Street. It billed itself as the world's largest department store. By any measure it was large, filling a square block and with nine stories of merchandise. Jack was one of approximately three hundred employees, an uncomfortable experience for him, for he had always worked in small stores with few fellow workers. Here he was only one of several shoe salesmen punching a time clock as he came and went.

Nelle soon took up her missions of mercy again and one afternoon had left Neil, seven, and "Dutch," four, alone for what she thought would be a short call on a neighbor. As the late afternoon shadows grew longer, the boys became frightened and decided to go in search of their mother. First, they blew out the gas lamp. On the street they encountered a friendly drunk who said they shouldn't be out so late. Just then, Nelle appeared. She had returned home to find it empty and filled with the smell of gas. She was frantic. Her usually sweet nature was replaced by real wrath visited upon the boys, followed by a "licking" by Jack when he came home from work.

In December, Jack lost his job. Whether it was a result solely of business conditions or partly because of his drinking is not known. What is known is that they packed up their belongings and took the train for Galesburg, a manufacturing city in northwestern Illinois.

The few months the family spent living in Chicago was the only time in Ronald Reagan's boyhood and youth spent outside of rural northwestern Illinois.

Chapter Three

Galesburg

Galesburg was not a random choice as a destination for the family. Jack had relatives there and felt sure they would help him get a job. They did. He became the shoe department manager of the O. T. Johnson Department Store.

Galesburg is a railroad and manufacturing city. Its population in 1910 was 22,089 and growing (today it is approximately 34,000). It is in Knox County, about forty miles west of Peoria. It was founded in 1835 by George Washington Gale, a Presbyterian minister whose dream was to create a vocational college. (He did, and it became Knox College.) He and a group from New York state purchased acreage that year for the creation of a town. The first two dozen settlers soon arrived. They built temporary log cabin shelters just north of the town limits, because Gale and his committee decided there would be no log cabins in the town.

In 1837, Galesburg saw the founding of the state's first antislavery society. The town soon became a stop on the "Underground Railway." One of the Lincoln-Douglas debates took place on the campus of Knox College in October 1858. Poet Carl Sandburg was born in Galesburg in 1878. Loyal Davis, who was to become Ronald Reagan's father-in-law in 1952 when Reagan married Nancy Davis, was born in Galesburg in 1896. He attended Knox College before earning his medical degree at Northwestern University's medical school. (He was chairman of the school's Department of Surgery for thirty-one years and served as a chairman and president of the American College of Surgeons. He died in 1982.)

As the railroads developed, Galesburg became an important point on their major east-west lines, the Chicago, Burlington and Quincy Railroad and the Atchison, Topeka and Santa Fe Railway. At one point, each had a station, and there was a major "sorting" yard for the Burlington line. (Today, as the Burlington Northern Santa Fe, the railroad still uses the yard. After the closing of a Maytag appliance plant in 2004, the BNSF became the city's largest employer.)

The Reagans Move into Town

Many Galesburg residential streets were shaded by large elms. The Reagans rented a brick house on one of these (1219 North Kellogg Street). Young Ron, then five, discovered in the attic a large collection of birds' eggs and butterflies, left there by the landlord. They fired his imagination. He wrote later, "Here, in the musty attic dust, I got my first scent of wind on peaks, pine needles in the rain, and visions of sunrise on the desert."[1]

Being a small boy, to him the new house seemed enormous, as did the empty lot across the street. To him it was an open field, where he could experience "nature in the raw" and watch a "shiny emerald-green grass snake."

One of the years back in Tampico, brother Neil's often-stated Christmas wish for an electric train had been met with Jack's fatherly expressions intended to dampen his expectations. Then, on Christmas morning, the wishes were fulfilled, despite the need for Jack and Nelle to cut back on the family's meat budget for at least two weeks. Now, Ron very much wanted to learn to ride Neil's secondhand bicycle, but said nothing. He would sit on the seat of the bike, holding on to a hitching post, at noontime when Jack returned for lunch. Jack would push him around the street for "a few exhilarating circles" each time, thus fulfilling another boy's wish.

Learning to Read

The Galesburg school did not have a kindergarten, so Nelle decided to "home school" Ronald by teaching him to read. Every evening she read books aloud. She followed each word with her finger, with the boys looking over her shoulder. As Ronald Reagan put it years later, "One evening all the funny black marks on paper clicked in place."[2]

At the time, he was lying on the floor, poring over the day's newspaper. Jack asked him what he was doing. "Reading," he replied. Jack then said, "Read me something," and he did. Nelle was so pleased with his accomplishment that she invited the neighbors in to hear him read the news about a bomb exploding in San Francisco during a parade and details of the "Black Tom" explosion in New Jersey.

In the fall of 1916, Dutch entered first grade at the Silas Willard School. The next spring, on April 6, 1917, the United States entered World War I. Jack answered the call for enlistees but learned at the army recruiting office that fathers of two or more children were not being accepted at that time.

Moving On

When it was time for Dutch to enter second grade, in September 1917, he was tested and was moved into the third grade. He seemed to have a photographic memory and did well in school, despite being very nearsighted.

In the middle of the 1917–18 school year Jack lost his job (again because of his occasional drinking binges), thus forcing the family to move once more. This time he was able to get a job as a shoe clerk at the E. B. Colwell Department Store in Monmouth, ten miles west of Galesburg.

Chapter Four

Monmouth

After the War of 1812, the federal government had offered land tracts to veterans as a bonus for their war service. In 1827, one veteran bet his section in the Illinois Military Tract in a New Orleans poker game, and lost. The winner was John Talbot, owner of a Kentucky plantation. Talbot and his cousin Allen Andrews went to Illinois to look over his land. Talbot liked it and constructed a one-room cabin about eight miles northeast of the present-day city of Monmouth.

Talbot sent word to friends back in Kentucky to come look over the land, and a group did in 1828. Their first order of business was to name the site of the new town. They put three names in a hat: "Kosciusko," "Isabella," and "Monmouth."

"Kosciusko" was the name drawn, but all decided that, despite honoring the Polish hero of the American Revolution, it would be too hard to spell and pronounce, so they drew again. This time it was "Monmouth," presumably after the Revolutionary War battle. Thus the town was founded in 1831 with this name.

In 1853, Monmouth Academy (which became Monmouth College in 1856) opened. In that decade the first of three railroad lines arrived. After the Civil War, good clay was discovered in the area, and several pottery companies were established.

Monmouth became the county seat of Warren County. In March 1878, the future western lawman Wyatt Earp was born in Monmouth.

The Reagans Make Monmouth Home

Jack and Nelle rented a two-story house at 218 Seventh Avenue, and Jack began his new job at the E. B. Colwell Department Store. Their house was near the campus of Monmouth College in a slightly hilly neighborhood—hilly enough for Dutch and Neil to go sledding in the winter.

As a seven-and-a-half-year-old, Dutch saw the local celebrations of the World War I armistice on November 11, 1918. As he wrote in his memoir, "The parades, torches, bands, shoutings, the drunks and burning Kaiser Bill in effigy gave me an uneasy feeling of a world outside my own."[1]

Not long afterward the flu epidemic that was sweeping the nation (and beyond) hit Monmouth, and Nelle fell victim to it. The school closed temporarily, and everyone who was not already ill wore a surgical mask. Nelle's condition worsened, and Jack thought she was going to die. He would confer with Dr. Laurence, then tell the boys she would be all right, but they weren't convinced. The doctor had an odd prescription in these pre-penicillin days. It was to keep her filled with green cheese, "the moldier the better." It worked. She gradually regained her health.

Once back on her feet, Nelle resumed and expanded her missionary work. She prayed constantly for Jack, hoping his drinking problem would abate, but she also prayed for members and their families in the local church. She was always ready to provide words of encouragement and solace to anyone in need of either. She had a clear reading and singing voice and knew many passages of the Bible by heart.

Dutch was doing well in the third grade, despite his nearsightedness, of which his parents were unaware. He assumed that everyone saw people at a distance only as blurs, without distinct features. His teacher, Miss Luhens, was impressed by the extent of his memory. He retained names and dates he had read about, and had memorized the multiplication tables.

Years later, classmate Gertrude Crockett noted Dutch Reagan's "'charisma'—everyone was taken with it."[2]

In the late winter of 1918–19 Ronald came down with pneumonia. The first day he was well enough to sit up, neighborhood boys who had ganged up on him when they first arrived in town brought their toy soldiers for him to play with.

By 1919, the postwar economy was improving, but Jack and Nelle were still having a hard time keeping their budget in balance. Nelle would stretch the food budget by making "oatmeal meat." She would knead oatmeal into a pound of ground beef, then make patties—thus doubling the life of that one pound of meat.

Most evenings were quiet, around the kitchen table, with Jack reading his newspaper and Nelle reading aloud to the boys about King Arthur and the knights of the Round Table or other tales of far-off adventure. On those evenings there was always a bowl of popcorn and a plate of apples.

In July of that year, H. C. Pitney, who had reacquired his store, wrote to Jack. Pitney was beginning to lose his eyesight and had no one to manage the store if he was sidelined. He offered Jack more pay than before and a chance to become a partner if he would return to Tampico.

Thus, in August the Reagan family moved once again to Tampico.

Chapter Five

Back to Tampico

All four of the Reagans were in high spirits when they arrived again in Tampico in August 1919. Jack was upbeat because he was leaving Monmouth for a better job in Tampico, rather than losing his job because of drinking. Nelle was happy for him and the likelihood that their money worries would end. The boys would soon be elated because of all the boyhood adventures that lay ahead of them.

This time, they moved into the apartment right above the Pitney store. Dutch soon gained a pal in Harold "Monkey" (or just plain "Monk") Winchell, who lived in the apartment above the store across the street that Monk's father owned. The boys communicated by signals from their respective windows. One Saturday evening Ronald visited Monkey (whose nickname came from his insatiable curiosity), ostensibly to study for Sunday school the next day.

Instead, Monkey had found his father's pump shotgun and had it out, in his bedroom. He put the butt of the gun on the floor and pulled the trigger, but there was silence. At that point, Dutch pumped the gun and handed it back to Monkey and asked him to try it again. He did, with a thunderous result. Plaster and lath began raining on the pair.

When their parents ran up the stairs, they found the two covered with plaster dust, but trying to appear to be reading their Sunday school lessons; however, their books were upside down.

Ronald Reagan later related that the licking he got from Jack didn't compare for sheer misery with the job of peeling a carload of secondhand potatoes Jack had purchased for the purpose of speculating. Dutch and Neil were assigned to the boxcar to peel the stinking spuds, many of which were rotting. They did it for several days but finally found the smell making them sick to their stomachs, so they ditched many of the potatoes. Jack apparently made a small profit from the salvaged ones he sold to local grocers.

Surrogate Grandparents

None of the Reagan boys' grandparents were living. Happily for the boys, their next-door neighbors, the Greenmans, a jeweler and his wife, were a childless older couple. "Aunt Emma," as they called Mrs. Greenman, gave Dutch ten cents a week as an allowance, plus cookies every afternoon. Dutch reveled in times spent in their living room, with its warm old furniture, sitting in a rocker, dreaming, and "Uncle Jim's" jewelry store with its cacophony of ticking clocks and bright gold and silver jewelry.

Nelle in Her Element

In addition to doing biblical recitations at church, Nelle began to develop a reputation for excellent dramatic recitals in town and the countryside nearby. Whether poetry, classic speeches, or passages from dramas, she enjoyed herself. At church, eight-year-old Dutch was pressed into service at one point to appear in a pageant in a sheet as "The Spirit of Christmas Never Was." Whether this ignited his interest in acting is not certain, but it was probably his first performance before an audience.

One passage from II Chronicles (7:14) became Nelle's favorite: "If my people who are called by my name humble themselves, and pray and seek my face, and turn from their wicked ways, then I will hear from heaven, and will forgive their sin and heal their land."

The First Football Games

Neil was better at the pickup football games they played in Tampico in those days, but not greater in enthusiasm than Dutch, who said, "I got a wild exhilaration out of jumping feet first into a pile-up."[1] Typically, the one boy among their group of friends who owned a football would begin the process of rounding up enough others in the neighborhood to start a game on a nearby field. Teams were chosen, and once the ball had been kicked off, both teams, it seemed, piled on the boy who was unlucky enough to have caught it. Thus began Ronald Reagan's lifelong love of football.

Seeing in Focus

One reason he was attracted to football was that he didn't need to have sharp focus in order to pile on an opposing ball carrier or stop a lineman from the other side. As for baseball, he shied from playing it, because he couldn't see the ball coming until it was almost upon him.

One Sunday the family was out for a drive (in a borrowed automobile). The others were talking about various sights. Ronald asked his mother if he could try on her eyeglasses. When he put them on, the world changed instantly and dramatically. He could read signs by the road and see features on the faces of people on the streets. He was amazed. He thought everyone saw things as he did—that is, that people not more than a few feet away had no features, and trees and other aspects of the landscape were fuzzy.

Apparently, neither Jack nor Nelle had noticed Ronald's nearsightedness. Because of his excellent memory he did well in school. Now Nelle realized why he always wanted to sit in the first row at the movies and read on the floor on his stomach, his eyes just inches from the book or newspaper.

After the revelation of Dutch's vision problem, Nelle took him to an optometrist and had him fitted for a pair of thick, black-rimmed glasses. He didn't like them, for he thought they made him look "bookish," but he did wear them most of the time. (Years later, in the early 1940s, when contact lenses were first being offered, he acquired a pair, and after that he used contacts for the rest of his life.)

Although his school grades were already good, they got better with his improved vision. This earned the approval of his stern but kindhearted third grade teacher, Miss Nellie Darby.

Despite his natural boy's interest in sports, outdoor games, and mock battles, Dutch loved to read. He read and dreamed of life as a dashing cowboy or sports star. As he grew older, the dreams dealt with more realistic pursuits. As time went on it was Nelle who gave him the drive, the tenacity to work to make his dreams come true.

More Adventures

On Saturdays, with Monk Winchell or Vernon "Newt" Denison, he would carry coal to the Opera House and straighten the chairs there so they could each earn ten cents to see the silent Western movies, especially those starring Tom Mix.

In summer, swimming was another favorite activity. Some local businessmen took a group of local boys to the Hennepin Canal to teach them to swim. Although Neil was bigger and built more like an athlete, and was a better football player, Ronald, who at that age was small and thin, was very competitive and constantly worked on improving his abilities. He soon excelled at swimming.

The local short-line railroad, nicknamed "The Dummy," was another source of adventure for boys. It made its way over a thirteen-mile course between Tampico and the smaller towns of Yorktown and Hooppole. It went forward in one direction, then had to back up to return, since there was no roundhouse turntable at the other end of the line to turn around the engine. The train, which carried passengers and freight, had a maximum speed of five miles per hour. The boys would jump aboard in Tampico and enact mock train robberies and play other make-believe games as The Dummy trundled toward its destinations—all to the amusement of the conductor and engineer.

Denison also recalled another game the boys played—this one at the local stockyards. They would choose teams, then play tag across the yards, swinging on the gates, opening and closing them to thwart the other team. If they failed, they were tagged and thus "it."

During the Christmas season that year they took the train to visit Nelle's brother and his wife, who lived on a farm near Morrison, Illinois. The boys had a new adventure: riding in a sleigh from the station to the farm through the snow, with hot bricks to warm their feet and buffalo robes to cover their legs.

The next summer, Dutch remembered, they rode in a fringed-top surrey to the farm. He began to talk about becoming a cowboy out west when he grew up. At the Denison farm they all took turns listening to the crystal radio set with earphones as the announcer would play music, then say, "This is KDKA, Pittsburgh."

Of Dutch Reagan in Tampico, his friend Vernon Denison said years later, "He was just a regular boy. . . . He liked sports. We'd play fox-and-goose in the snow. He'd forget his mittens and overshoes. He was just like the rest of us. They'd had their family problems, just like the rest of us."[2]

The Glassburn family lived just outside town and had a horse. On his visits to their place, Dutch fell in love with horseback riding, a love that lasted a lifetime. Many times in later years he would say, "There is nothing better for the inside of a man than the outside of a horse."

Stanley Glassburn, asked about his childhood friend after Reagan was elected president, said Dutch was well-liked by his friends and was always a leader of the group.

Monk Winchell recalled, "We were poor folks, but [Dutch] and Neil were always dressed clean, not raggedy."[3] Reagan said, many years later, "We were poor, but so was everyone else we knew so it didn't seem as if we were poor."

Now in his ninth and tenth years, for Ronald Reagan the elements of self-reliance and leadership were already taking root, from earning money to go to the movies, to leading, barefoot, his gang of pals to the canal for a swim

Jack and Prohibition

At one minute after midnight on January 16, 1920, the bells pealed at the Disciples of Christ church to celebrate the beginning of Prohibition, as the Volstead Act went into effect. The town's one tavern closed. This had been Jack's Saturday night outlet, where he could exchange yarns with other men and drink and talk of better times.

This outlet was no longer available to him, although "near beer" was still sold. This was beer that had virtually all its alcohol removed. One could add a few drops of "medicinal" alcohol to it to get the desired "buzz."

Regardless of the method by which Jack drank, he did so more or less in direct proportion to his dissatisfaction with his job. Although this was increasing, he did not show it to his customers. Years later, Gordon Glassburn, a third-grade classmate of Dutch's, said, "Everybody went there [to Pitney's] because of Jack. There was no nicer man than Jack Reagan when he wasn't drinking."

He added that "Dutch got his talent from his mother and his personality from his father. . . . I used to run around with Neil years ago. Dutch didn't do much running around. He sat on a porch, reading a book. He was different from Neil. Neil had a lot of zip. Neil was a talker. He chewed gum just as hard. Neil was full of the devil."

Jean Kinney, a lifelong friend of Neil, said, "Neil seemed always to be defying his mother. I had the feeling he . . . preferred to think he was like his father."[4] To Neil, Jack represented laughter and good stories. Nelle, on the other hand, represented much praying and the setting of high standards of behavior.

Despite her church's firm opposition to alcohol and Nelle's frequent and fervent prayers for the Lord to deliver Jack from his demon, she held and expressed the view that alcoholism was a disease and that its victims should not be blamed. She thus forgave Jack for his Saturday binges.

Nelle seemed to gravitate most to her younger son. She often took him with her to her church dramatic group's meetings and readings. He had absorbed her lessons about good manners, and he was thus a favorite of her women friends. Gladys Glassburn Pierce, another third-grade classmate of Dutch's, reminisced years later that "his mother was really a Christian. She was what you call 'lady.'"

A New Opportunity

In late 1920, Mr. Pitney decided once again to sell the store. From what he had said earlier, Jack, as manager, expected to get a percentage of the sale price. Instead, Pitney offered him a percentage of another store he owned, the Fashion Boot Shop in Dixon, twenty-six miles away. He said Jack would manage this store.

Warren Harding had just been elected president. Ever since President Woodrow Wilson's stroke in 1919, the country seemed to be holding back on optimism. Now, with a new president coming in, the future looked open and bright. Despite Jack's disappointment about the proceeds of the Tampico store sale, he said yes to Pitney's offer. Jack, who enjoyed fitting and selling shoes more than any other aspect of the dry goods business, saw this as the opportunity for success he was really looking for. The family prepared to move once again.

In their first automobile, purchased used from Pitney, the Reagan family left Tampico on December 6, 1920, with most of their belongings lashed to the top of the car. Jack had decreed that the boys' cat and her three new kittens could not go with them; however, Nelle tucked them all into a basket, covered it with a blanket, and put it on the floor of the back seat under Neil's and Ronald's feet. All week before the trip the boys were tantalized by Jack's tales of life in "the big city" of Dixon, where the circus visited, where there were many more people than in Tampico, and where they would have a house with its own yard for the boys to play in.

(In 1919 the owners of the First National Bank of Tampico purchased the building that included the apartment where Ronald Reagan was born and moved the bank into the ground-floor commercial space. The bank did not survive the Depression. Later, the Tampico City Hall occupied the space. Reagan returned to Tampico three times in later years: in 1950, when he and Nelle were grand marshals of the Homecoming Parade that summer; in January 1976, when Reagan was campaigning for the Republican presidential nomination and led the press corps to his upstairs birthplace, as well as having a reunion with his third-grade classmates at the local school; and in 1992 when he and his wife, Nancy, visited the town on Mother's Day, attended services in the Disciples of Christ Church, and had lunch at the "Dutch" Diner.)

Dixon

Many small midwestern cities with manufacturing saw growth between 1910 and 1920. Dixon, Illinois, logged 7,216 residents in 1910 and 8,191 in 1920 (by 2000 it was 15,941). Surrounded by deep, rich soil given to dairy farming and raising wheat and corn, the small city itself had several factories when the Reagans arrived: J. I. Case, which made farm implements; the Reynolds Wire Company; the Medusa Cement Company; and the Clipper Lawn Mower Company. About half of Dixon's population was employed in industry. Most of the dairy farms were suppliers to the Borden Milk Company.

Because it was not close to any large metropolitan area (Chicago, to the east, was nearly one hundred miles away, as was Peoria, to the south), Dixon was more or less isolated and therefore self-contained. People tended to live their entire lives there. Although the town was built on low hills, there was no hilltop of great houses. Even the most prosperous merchants and professional men of the day lived in frame houses, much like their neighbors.

It was a middle-class to lower-middle-class town from an income point of view. The homes and yards were tidy but unpretentious. Dixon had one movie theater, a small playhouse, and a golf course. It also had a newspaper, the *Dixon Evening Telegraph*.

Bisected by the swift Rock River, Dixon was oriented to this feature in both summer and winter. The river is about three-eighths of a mile wide as it courses through the city. Lowell Park, on the west shore and about two miles north of the city, was a site for swimming, boating, picnicking, and fishing. Up the river a mile or so was the Chautauqua park, dominated by the Assembly Building, a large circular shed with open sides, in which for two or three weeks every summer the nationwide Chautauqua circuit booked church conclaves and lecturers. Out-of-town visitors would camp on the grounds of the park, and there were many food and beverage concessionaires to serve them. (Years later, the Assembly Building burned to the ground one night, never to be restored.)

In 1920 both the Northwestern and Illinois Central railroads came through Dixon. This benefited the area's farmers, who could easily ship to Omaha, Chicago, or southern markets from Dixon.

History's Westward March

The restless urge of Americans to press westward for land and opportunity was at work in northwestern Illinois in the 1820s, as it was in many other places. In the early days, many had Galena as their destination. In the northwestern corner of the state, Galena is on the river of the same name (navigable then, but no longer), about two miles from the Mississippi. Early Indian tribes dug lead ore from the soil and used it as body paint. In the 1690s French trappers discovered the area and began to mine lead.

By 1816, George Davenport, a retired army colonel, settled in the area and began a thriving lead business, shipping his first boatload down the Mississippi in 1816. By 1845 Galena and its county were producing 80 percent of the lead in the United States.

Many of the pioneers bound for this new lead bonanza were coming overland from the east, and Dixon offered a direct route northwest to Galena. Dixon is about ninety-five miles from Galena as the crow flies, but these travelers were not crows, but people on foot. They had to ford the swift and dangerous Rock River in order to make the final trek to Galena.

In 1828 a French-Canadian trapper, Joseph Ogee, made the trek easier (and himself some good money) by inaugurating a ferry service to haul wagons, draft animals, and pioneers across the river. He also owned a tavern to slake the thirst and hunger of the travelers.

After two years, Ogee cashed out by selling his business and his cabin to John Dixon. By April 11, 1830, Dixon had sent for his family to join him. He had the name "Dixon's Ferry" bestowed on the tiny settlement's new post office. The Rock River Indians called Dixon *Nada-chu-ra-sak* (White-haired Father).

As Galena grew, so did Dixon, but once the demand for lead from the former declined, in the later part of the nineteenth century, Dixon's own growth slowed to a trickle (it added only 1,216 new residents in the fifty years between 1860 and 1910). It was becoming a farming, then a farming-manufacturing town.

Lincoln in Dixon

Beginning in 1830, Chief Black Hawk, to avenge the loss of his birthplace by means of disputed treaties with the U.S. government, began a series of forays into western Illinois. In the early ones he was persuaded to leave without any blood being shed. In 1832, however, he had promises of alliances from other tribes (which did not materialize) and expected to get assistance from the British.

On April 5, with about a thousand warriors, he invaded Illinois in earnest. Several skirmishes ensued, including the battle of Stillman's Run. The Illinois and Wisconsin militias were mobilized to hunt, capture, or disperse Black Hawk's band.

The governor put out a call for volunteers. Abraham Lincoln, who was living in New Salem at the time (about 120 miles west of Springfield), had just announced his candidacy for the Illinois House of Representatives. The election would not be held until later in the year, so on April 21 Lincoln rode to Beardstown to join a company of volunteers. They were sworn in. An election for company captain was held, and Lincoln won.

On April 30 he was commissioned a captain in the Thirty-first Regiment of Militia of Sangamon County, First Division. He was in charge of a rifle company of the Fourth Regiment of Mounted Volunteers. Despite the long titles, these soldiers had a great deal of marching ahead of them.

Early May was spent supplying and resupplying themselves on their march toward the mouth of the Rock River. They reached Dixon's Ferry and set up camp on May 12. Shortly thereafter Lincoln led his company to the site of the battle of Stillman's Run. They found dead soldiers, scalped and mutilated. They buried them.

On May 27 Lincoln's company was mustered out of service. The next day, he enlisted—as a private—in Captain Elijah Iles's company. Iles had turned a group of seventy-one former officers into a mounted company in Ottawa, Illinois. They proceeded to Dixon's Ferry on June 7 and a day later headed to Galena, but did not see action. They returned to Dixon's Ferry on the thirteenth and were mustered out of service on the sixteenth.

That same day, Lincoln enlisted as a private in Captain Jacob Early's independent company (meaning it operated separately from the brigade). The company remained at Dixon's Ferry until the twenty-sixth, when it was sent to the site of the battle of Kellogg's Grove to bury the dead. The company then returned to Dixon's Ferry, where it remained until July 10. At that time, the brigade's leaders decided they had more men than they needed, so they mustered out all of Early's company, ending Lincoln's military career less than three months after it had begun. During that time he saw no combat, but contemporaries generally regarded him as an able and competent soldier and leader.

As for Black Hawk, U.S. troops dispersed and eliminated many of his warriors. He and a few other leaders escaped; however, they later surrendered and spent a year in prison.

(Lincoln's brief stays in Dixon are commemorated by a statue of him as a twenty-three-year-old volunteer, in Presidents' Park on the city's north shore of the Rock River, on the site of the Black Hawk War–era Fort Dixon. Lincoln returned to Dixon on July 17, 1856, to the grounds of the Lee County Courthouse to deliver a long campaign speech on behalf of the Republican Party's first presidential candidate, John C. Frémont. A plaque at the site commemorates the visit.)

The Reagans Arrive

Once Pitney's sale of the Tampico store was a certainty, Jack had taken a day off to go to Dixon to see about renting a house. He had signed a lease for a two-story clapboard house at 816 South Hennepin Avenue (on the south side of the Rock River). Built in 1891, it was now owned by John and Teresa Donovan. Mrs. Donovan had inherited it. Jack had paid the first month's rent, twenty-three dollars, then returned to Tampico to tell Nelle and the boys about it.

As they entered Dixon on December 6, Jack decided to give the family a tour of downtown. They drove north on Galena, the main street, under the fairly new Memorial Arch, a wooden structure that spanned the street. It was to be permanent, replacing a temporary arch that had been erected to honor the town's returning servicemen after the Armistice in 1918. The arch proclaimed in large letters: DIXON. (Many such temporary arches were constructed in towns throughout the nation. Only a few survive, and Dixon's has long since been replaced by a replica made of steel and concrete.)

After driving through the commercial district and the riverfront, the Reagans found Hennepin Avenue and their new home. The rooms were not large, but the house had three bedrooms, an indoor toilet, a parlor, adjacent family living room, dining room, and kitchen. It also had a fireplace.

One bedroom was to be Jack and Nelle's, the one next to it, the boys' room, and the third, Nelle's sewing room. In it she could use her new Singer sewing machine. And, thinking about financial security, she and Jack saw it as a room that they could rent out if it became necessary. Nelle ordered from the Sears, Roebuck catalog a cabinet to hold the china she had been given as a wedding present.

A few yards behind the house was a small barn, large enough to be a garage for the family's Ford Model T and with a loft for the boys to use as a "clubhouse."

Jack's High Hopes Meet Reality

Jack's dream of owning a shop of his own was to come true in Dixon. Hadn't Mr. Pitney promised him a half interest in his Dixon store, and wouldn't Pitney be retiring before long? All the signs looked good. The reality was different. What Mr. Pitney had in mind was to credit any commissions Jack earned toward the value of a half interest in the store. The ownership of the half interest would not be transferred to him on paper until he had earned it this way. That left only Jack's modest base salary for the family to live on.

Jack had little understanding of the processes of business management and did not know what questions he should have asked. Although he was naive, he trusted in what he was told and was thus embittered by what he thought was an unfair deal he had gotten from Pitney.

This did not solve the family's immediate budget problems. Nelle, resourceful as usual, went back to her standby, oatmeal meat, and asked the butcher for some liver for the cat (thrown in with the rest of the order at no charge). She also bought soup bones. She made one last for a week as soup, with potatoes, onions, and carrots added. As the week went on, she added more water, potatoes, and vegetables. The onions and carrots came from a small vegetable garden they had planted. She also harvested onions to cook with a slab of bacon and the free liver for Sunday dinner. (The cats didn't miss the liver, since the barn had plenty of mice for them.)

Early School Days

The Reagan brothers were enrolled in South Central School, Neil in the seventh grade and Dutch in the second half of the fifth grade. Schoolmates soon gave Neil the nickname "Moon," after the comic

pages' Moon Mullins. Moon made new friends more quickly and easily than Dutch, but they both lost no time becoming friends with the
O'Malley brothers, George and Ed, who lived across the street. This
soon led to impromptu football games, with the older boys, George
and Moon, opposing Dutch and Ed.

Nearly every afternoon from late summer until the first snowfall,
they played. One team consisted of the center and the ball carrier;
the other, the defense. They played on the O'Malleys' lawn until it
seemed to be getting chewed up. Then they would move to the lawn
on the side of the Reagans' house for a while, then back again to the
O'Malleys'.

Moon was a better player than his brother, but Dutch had the
same fierce enthusiasm for the game he had had in Tampico. Ed
O'Malley recalled that "Dutch was a bit nearsighted, but he always
wanted to carry the ball." He would pass it to Dutch, who "would
go charging ahead." The older boys—the opposing team—would
let him begin his charge, "when they would trip him, sending him
flying into the bushes."[1] Dutch, just ten in 1921, was still small and
lightweight.

Each year, as fall edged into winter and football playing came
to an end, Dutch longed for the winter freeze to come—but without
snow—so he could skate on the Rock River. He described it as "a
rink two hundred yards wide and endlessly long, as clear and smooth
as glass." His greatest pleasure then was to "skate for miles," then
turn and spread his coat open so the wind would blow him back to
the starting point. His small size and light weight was an advantage

in the impromptu games of "assassination hockey" he played with his friends. Its object was to skate furiously to avoid being tagged. "It made me an excellent skater," he later wrote.[2]

At the Movies

Like just about everyone else, Dutch loved the movies. His list of favorites was headed by Westerns featuring Tom Mix and William S. Hart as they caught villains and saved beautiful girls. Later he added to the list sports films in which star athletes of the day showed off their talents.

Often the whole family went to the movies on Friday evening. If Dutch could persuade his father to give him a dime the next day, he could see the Saturday matinee. One Saturday it was D. W. Griffith's *Birth of a Nation*. Among other things, it had scenes that included post–Civil War Ku Klux Klan members. By the early 1920s the Klan had established some chapters in the Midwest and was spreading its anti-black message, along with anti-Jewish and anti-Catholic prejudice.

When Dutch asked Jack if he could have a dime to see the film that everyone seemed to be talking about, he got a taste of Jack's strong feelings about prejudice. Jack said, "The Klan's the Klan, and a sheet's a sheet, and any man who wears a sheet over his head is a bum. And I want no more words on the subject."[3] Dutch did not see the film.

Soon after the move to Dixon, Dutch took out a library card—number 3695—at the Dixon Public Library. From then on, nearly every weekend he visited the library and took out an average of two books a week, usually adventure tales that stirred a boy's imagination.

Jack's "Weakness"

One late-winter day in early 1922, when Dutch was just eleven, he came home to find his father passed out—drunk—on the front porch. After he stood there watching for a minute or two, his impulse was to go into the house, head straight upstairs and to bed—pretending this had not happened. He was aware of Jack's "weakness" for alcohol, from his occasional long absences, and loud voices late in the night. Yet he had been insulated, for his mother always seemed to handle these situations. This time, he wrote later, "I felt myself filled with grief for my father and the same time I was feeling sorry for myself. Seeing his arms spread out as if they were crucified—as indeed he was—his hair soaked with melting snow, snoring as he breathed ... I bent over him, smelling the sharp odor. . . . I got a fistful of his overcoat. Opening the door, I managed to drag him inside and get him to bed."[4]

This had a lasting effect on Ronald Reagan. As his life and career moved forward, his public personality was that of a person unfailingly polite and affable, but his private personality was one in which he kept feelings to himself.

He liked his father, despite the weakness. He subscribed to his mother's view to always look for the good in people and not to condemn them for something over which they had little or no control.

He enjoyed his father's sense of humor, his ribald jokes, and his belief that all people were created equal and that what a person did with his ambition determined how far he would go. (Years later, Ronald Reagan's frequent arguments for equality of opportunity stemmed from this lesson he learned from his father.) Jack was deeply opposed to racial and ethnic prejudice. As an example, Dutch wrote about an experience a few years later, during the Depression, when Jack was a traveling shoe salesman. He checked into a small town's hotel and signed the register. The clerk said, "You'll like it here, Mr. Reagan. We don't permit a Jew in the place." Thereupon, Jack picked up his suitcase and said, "I'm a Catholic. . . . and if it comes to the point where you won't take Jews, you won't take me either." He stormed out. As it was the town's only hotel, he slept in his car in the snow.[5]

The Barn

Dutch began to collect bird's eggs. Jack had an unused display case at the store and brought it home to the barn loft. Dutch would climb tree after tree and retrieve eggs, put a small hole in each end, then blow the egg out. He would then label the empty shell and put it in the glass display case.

Moon's interest was more business oriented. He raised pigeons and rabbits in the barn. On occasional Fridays he would kill some squabs and rabbits, skin them and clean them, then tuck them in a market basket and the next day sell them all in the neighborhood.

The brothers went their own way with their interests but were always ready to stick up for one another. In Dixon school days, Moon, being older and bigger, took the lead. The roles were to reverse a few years later.

Church Work Begins

Nelle had joined the Disciples of Christ Church in Dixon by letter before they left Tampico. When the Reagans arrived, the church was holding its services at the YMCA, having sold its building in 1917 to the Loyal Order of Moose. It met variously at the Dixon Armory, the First Baptist Church, and the YMCA until June 19, 1921, when it first held services in its new building, which it purchased from the Universalist Society of Dixon. The initial services were held in the basement because restoration work was still being done on the sanctuary as a result of serious fire damage in late 1917.

In early 1921 Nelle was appointed teacher of the church's True Blue Sunday School class, a position she held for the next sixteen years. During those first months when services were held at the YMCA, Neil and Ronald attended with Nelle but also became interested in YMCA programs. Dutch joined its marching band as drum major. Moon soon joined its high school unit that served at small rural church services that might otherwise not have had anyone to conduct them.

This was at a time when there was a widespread Midwest revival in "fundamentalism" in religion. The Christian Church (Disciples of Christ) described its own beliefs as "liberal fundamentalism." The fundamentals of belief to which it adhered were infallibility of the

Bible; the virgin birth of Jesus Christ; his death in order to atone for the sins of the world; his resurrection; and his Second Coming.

Although tithing was not considered obligatory by the Disciples of Christ, it was with Nelle. No matter the state of family finances, she insisted on setting aside one-tenth of their income to support the church. Jack was often unhappy about this but nevertheless agreed. Also, anything the boys earned was considered part of the family's income, so subject to tithing. It was a lesson in self-discipline Dutch never forgot.

That Printer of Udell's

One spring day in 1922, Dutch came across a copy of *That Printer of Udell's: A Story of the Middle West*, by Harold Bell Wright, which Nelle had left on the table in the family living room.

Wright was a very popular novelist in the early part of the twentieth century, specializing in tales of inspiration and moral uplift. *That Printer of Udell's*, first published in 1902, sold more than a million copies. The story revolves around Dick Falkner. He works as a printer but also attends night school to better himself. He then saves a beautiful woman from falling into prostitution. It turns out she is a socialite. They marry. He goes on to improve the life of their town through Christian and business principles. At the conclusion he has been elected to Congress and is off to Washington to uplift the nation.

As a boy of eleven, Reagan was deeply moved by this book. Years later he said, "All in all, as I look back, I realize that my reading left an abiding belief in the triumph of good over evil." Soon after he read the book, he told his mother that he wanted to declare his faith and be baptized.[6] On June 21, 1922, the Reverend David Franklin Seyster baptized both Ronald and Neil Reagan, as part of a group of twenty-five. (Neil later moved to the local Catholic church.)

There was only one place in the church building for the Sunday school class, the furnace room. It was dark and cluttered. Dutch Reagan asked their teacher, Lloyd Emmert, for permission to refurbish it. He gave it, and Dutch led his classmates in a project that resulted in plastering and painting the room. He became a Sunday school teacher himself and led a class until it was time to leave for college in 1928.

He was popular with his Sunday school students, for he often told of well-known sports figures who actively applied Christian principles in their lives.

Interspersed with her visits to prisoners in the county jail and shut-ins and hospital patients, Nelle headed a group of about two dozen church women in the True Blue class. They met in members' homes to read and discuss the Bible and share experiences of how it had helped in their lives. When the meetings were held at the Reagan home, Dutch usually participated.

Not long after the death of the Disciples of Christ pastor the Reverend Harvey Garland Waggoner, three weeks before Dutch and Moon's baptism, a new pastor arrived, the Reverend Ben H. Cleaver. He began stopping by the True Blue meetings and, when at the Reagans' home, built a friendship with Dutch. In fact, in time he became an important sounding board for things on young Ron's mind.

Chautauqua Days

At the end of the Dixon streetcar line there was a park on the river dominated by the large open-sided Chautauqua shed. Named for a New York state town where it originated, the Chautauqua circuit was a national organization that offered lectures—most inspired by religious and uplifting themes—during a two- or three-week period each summer. It also organized church seminars. The big shed was surrounded by camping areas and the concessionaire booths.

During their first four or five years in Dixon, Dutch would usually accompany Nelle on her excursions to hear the Chautauqua shows. They would eat a light picnic, then attend. Dutch relished these occasions, for during them he learned the details of her many activities to make the world a better place.

Dutch liked his father's love of stories and jokes, but Jack had a cynical turn of mind, partly as a result of the various disappointments he had faced (and probably, disappointment in himself). Nelle, on the other hand, exuded optimism, and it constantly rubbed off on Dutch. He was leading a happy life in Dixon and was confident life ahead would be good. After all, as Nelle often told him, everything is part of God's plan.

Ronald Reagan as a baby (photo courtesy of Ronald Reagan Presidential Library and Foundation)

Left: The young Reagan family
(from left) Jack, Neil, Ronald, Nelle
(photo courtesy of Ronald Reagan
Birthplace, Tampico, Illinois)

Below: Reagan's fifth-grade classroom at the South Dixon Central
School (photo by the author)

Reagan's boyhood home on South Hennepin Avenue in Dixon (photo by the author)

First Christian Church (Disciples of Christ), Dixon, Illinois, where Nelle, Neil, and Ronald Reagan worshipped (photo courtesy of Ron Marlowe and Loveland Museum, Dixon, Illinois)

Acting in *Captain Applejack* at Dixon High School; Reagan is fourth from left, in tuxedo (photo courtesy of Ronald Reagan Presidential Library and Foundation)

Opposite page top: A postcard view of the Rock River at Lowell Park in Dixon. "Dutch" Reagan was the lifeguard at the Lowell Park beach for seven seasons (courtesy of Loveland Museum, Dixon, Illinois)

Drum major (at far left) of the YMCA marching band in Dixon (photo courtesy of Ronald Reagan Presidential Library and Foundation)

Eureka College's administration building, Burrus Dickenson Hall, built in the 1870s (courtesy of Eureka College Archives)

A standout swimmer on the Eureka College team (courtesy of Eureka College Archives)

In *The Art of Being Bored*: Reagan is seated; Margaret Cleaver is on the left (photo courtesy of Eureka College Archives)

The Eureka College Chapel, where Ronald Reagan first found his political voice during a student strike in 1928 (photo courtesy of Eureka College Archives)

Reagan on the starting Eureka football team (photo courtesy of Eureka College Archives)

Ralph McKinzie, athletic director and football coach at Eureka College while Reagan was a student there (photo courtesy of Eureka College Archives)

Behind the microphone as a WHO radio sportscaster, 1933 (photo courtesy of WHO Radio, Des Moines, Iowa)

As an officer trainee in the cavalry reserve at Camp Dodge, Reagan learned to be an expert rider; this photo was taken on his first ranch in the late 1940s (photo courtesy Boyd Melvin and Loveland Museum, Dixon, Illinois)

The residents of Dixon, Illinois, erected this equestrian statue of Reagan on the shores of the Rock River (photo by the author)

Chapter Seven

Across the River

In the summer of 1923, the family moved again. They could no longer afford the rent at the Hennepin Avenue house, so they moved to a smaller one on the north side of the river, at 338 West Everett Street. Gone was the barn with room for Dutch's collection of birds' eggs and Moon's rabbit and pigeon business. The boys shared a sleeping porch as their bedroom.

By then, Dixon had divided its high school into two campuses, North and South. At this time, Moon was about to enter his junior year, so he continued at South Dixon through to graduation. Dutch, just about to begin high school, enrolled at North Dixon. Soon, the two campuses were tagged with stereotyped labels. South Dixon was seen as more sports-oriented, rougher, while North Dixon was typecast as more interested in "culture." Years later, Moon said he and his friends considered the North Dixon boys "sissies." He would hint that he and his friends were well acquainted with Demon Town, that area on the waterfront where there were pool halls and speakeasies.

Dutch was still small for his age, five-foot-three and 108 pounds. Moon was an extrovert, while Dutch was content to spend hours reading. He had much less to say at the dinner table than did Moon; however, in public he was unfailingly polite, had a warm smile, and always looked people in the eye when he spoke with them. He welcomed the move to the North Dixon campus, for he had a crush on Margaret "Mugs" Cleaver, a bright, witty, and good-looking daughter of the Reverend Cleaver of the Disciples of Christ.

Moon played end on the Dixon football team. Dutch went out for football and attended every practice session, but sat out the first two seasons on the bench. He admired a senior varsity member, Winston "Wink" McReynolds, a son of one of Dixon's twelve black families. The two had become good friends, and Wink was a frequent visitor at the Reagans' home.

It was in the middle of his third football season, during the pre-game talk in the locker room as the coach announced the starting lineup, that finally Dutch's name was called as the right guard. All of his listening, watching, and learning had paid off.

Dutch also went out for basketball and made the team. During one basketball tournament in which the Dixon team played in a distant town, the team needed to stay the night. Wink McReynolds was one of Dutch's and Moon's teammates. The town's hotel said they did not allow blacks. So the Reagan brothers took him up the back stairs, and the trio shared a bed.

When Dutch went out for swimming, it was one sport where he was far better than Moon. He was unafraid of the water, didn't need 20–20 vision, and with his light frame he could slice through the water easily. He was soon swimming the Rock River, which had a well-deserved reputation as being dangerous because of its swift current. There had been many drownings in it over the decades.

A Sudden Spurt

In 1925, when he was fourteen, Dutch Reagan experienced the full force of puberty. His height increased (by his senior year he was six-foot-one), he began to "fill out," and he developed the muscles of a swimmer. He was also popular because of his sports activities. Although he was not the player his brother was, he was liked for his courage and determination on the field. In the 1926 football season, Moon's last, Dixon went undefeated. In 1928, Dutch's last, it won only two and lost seven.

In his junior year Dutch tried out for—and won—the lead male role in the Philip Barry play *You and I*. Margaret Cleaver played the female lead. By their senior year they were "steadies," seen virtually everywhere together.

By his senior year, Reagan was tall, handsome, friendly—a Big Man on Campus. He was elected senior class president at North Dixon. In the school yearbook, under his class photo, he chose as his motto a line from a poem he had written: "Life is just one grand, sweet song, so start the music." The full poem, "Life," was a paean to the optimism of youth.

Summer Jobs

Dutch's summer excursions to the Chautauqua with Nelle ended in 1924, for the next year he got his first summer job. It was with a building contractor who had a contract to construct St. Anne's Catholic Church. Young Ron's pay was thirty-five cents an hour. The work schedule was ten hours a day, six days a week. His first job was to dig the foundation for the building. One day, when the noon whistle blew, instead of setting down the pick, he let it drop over his back. It landed within a few inches of the boss's toes. (Jack was standing by, waiting to take Dutch home for lunch). The contractor yelled, "This kid of yours [is so lazy he] can get less dirt on a shovel than any human being that's human."[1] Despite his blooper, Dutch wasn't fired and had earned $200 by the end of the summer. All of this would be put away toward college.

Also, in 1925, before his construction job started, he and Moon became roustabouts for the Ringling Brothers Circus when it came to town for several days. They each earned twenty-five cents an hour pulling circus wagons into the mud so they wouldn't go down the slope into the river. They also had to report for work at 4 a.m. to feed the elephants.

In the spring of 1926, the city's park commission was seriously considering closing Lowell Park to summer swimming in the aftermath of several recent drownings. Dutch, who had taken a lifesaving course at the YMCA, thought that what was needed was a full-time, skilled lifeguard to provide the necessary measure of safety. He applied to the park concessionaires, Ed and Ruth Graybill, for the job.

Ruth Graybill was a member of the Disciples of Christ who had a favorable impression of young Ron. Nevertheless, she was concerned that he might be too young. Jack assured her that Ron could do the job. He knew that his son was an excellent swimmer and had taken the lifesaving class. Ruth was also aware that their concession license was at stake, so she hired Ron for eighteen dollars a week and all the root beer he could drink and dime hamburgers he could eat. His duties began at ten each morning and did not end until ten at night. After that, he cleaned up around the beach (the area was floodlit) before going home.

To start the day, he went to the Graybills' nearby house to get their truck so he could pick up the day's food supplies and a three-hundred-pound block of ice. He would break up the ice and put it into several coolers. Then he and Ruth Graybill would drive out to the park. For that summer and six more, Lowell Park would be his daily "home."

Lowell Park

In 1907 the family of the poet James Russell Lowell gave the city of Dixon a three-hundred-acre forested tract fronting on the Rock River for use as a public park. Since then, Lowell Park has been kept largely in a natural state. If you were to visit today, you would take the same winding road from the entrance down to the beach, much as Ronald Reagan did in his lifeguard days. The trees are taller now, and the forest is a little denser, but it is the same forest.

In Dutch Reagan's days, there was a dock out from the shore. It had a lower and an upper diving board (which also had a slide). A little farther out was a float—a goal for swimmers to reach. Safety lines were designed to keep people from trying to swim to the other shore, about two hundred yards away. Whenever the downstream dam's sluice gates were opened, it sharply increased the speed of the current, making it dangerous.

As Reagan later wrote, "The bottom sloped swiftly into deeper water not too far from the edge. . . . Swimming across was a challenge . . . once started you had to go all the way, or else. I learned . . . to watch for the unexpected, but to keep my eye mainly on the two or three places where trouble would begin: downstream from the dock or between dock and raft."[2]

Daring young men would go down the slide next to the upper diving board in "cannonball" fashion to see how big a splash they could make. One day, fifteen-year-old Gertrude Childers was next to the dock under the slide. She was just pushing out to swim to the float when a young man came down the slide with a whoosh and landed on top of her. Years later, she recalled, "I remember going under, but that's about all I remember because it knocked me out."[3] The next thing she remembered was waking up with a bad nosebleed. Dutch Reagan had saved her.

Altogether, he saved seventy-seven people over the years he worked at Lowell Park. To commemorate these, each time he made a rescue he cut a notch in an old log at the edge of the beach. In later years he was often asked if, in some cases, pretty girls hadn't feigned danger in order to be "rescued" by the handsome, muscular lifeguard. His reply: "I guarantee you they needed saving—no lifeguard gets wet without good reason."[4]

Reagan said that few of those rescued thanked him. Many were embarrassed at their predicament and insisted they would have been fine without him. In all those years, he received only one "thank you" tip, from an elderly man who had lost his upper plate when he went down the slide. Dutch dove for it and found it.

The Lowell Park beach in those days was very popular in the summer. A typical weekend day might see as many as a thousand people there, many of them young. In addition to swimming and socializing in the sun, visitors could picnic and walk on trails through the woods.

In 1909 Woodcote Lodge was built. On the ground floor was the Great Room, where, from about 1914, Ruth Graybill served dinner to the public. On weekends there was often improvised entertainment by musicians, actors, and artists coming out from

Chicago. By the early 1920s several cabins had been built, and these were rented for weeks at a time as summer retreats for families from Chicago and other cities.

Dutch, sometimes with a pal accompanying him, would teach children of summer cabin residents to swim. John Crabtree related one incident in an October 8, 1980, article in the *Wall Street Journal*: "I never head him cuss and the only time I knew him to take a drink was [when] this family . . . gave us each a bottle of homemade wine for helping teach their kids to swim. We finished the wine and [later] took a stroll through town. In those days the stoplights were on top of short cement posts . . . in the middle of the intersections. Dutch . . . climbed up on one . . . and sat there.

"The police chief came along in his Model T and asked Dutch what he was doing.

"'Twinkle, twinkle, little star, just who do you think you are,' said Dutch. The chief took him in and fined him a buck."

Margaret Cleaver first took real notice of Dutch Reagan when he became a lifeguard. Her best friend, Elizabeth "Bee" Drew, was ahead of them in school by a year. Late in the day, when the crowds had thinned, the two girls, along with Bee's boyfriend, would go to the park in their white canoe. To get a little free time to join the canoeing party, Dutch would skip pebbles across the river, then tell the few swimmers still around that it was a river rat. That caused the swimmers to leave.

Dutch got in the canoe, along with his portable Victrola (which seemed to play only "Ramona"), and off they went for a half-hour cruise.

Moving On in School

Moon graduated from Dixon High in 1926. He was not interested in going to college. Instead he got a job at a cement plant, making enough each month to contribute to the family's budget. When he was eighteen he decided to become a Catholic. When he told his mother, she told him that that was how he had been baptized a few days after his birth.

Dutch had learned to keep his feelings about Jack's binges to himself, while folding into his public personality the lessons he had learned from Nelle about positive attitudes, good manners, and solicitude toward others.

In addition to his drive and determination to do well in football, basketball, and swimming, his youthful experiences participating in some of Nelle's biblically related dramatic presentations had sparked his interest in the school's drama club.

B. J. Fraser was a young, outgoing teacher of English and world history and was the Dramatic Club's adviser. He encouraged Dutch to join. No arm-twisting was needed, as Margaret Cleaver was already a member. Fraser said of him, "He possessed a sense of presence on the stage, a sense of reality. . . . He fit into almost any role you put him into."[5]

Until then, the club's presentations were only to the student body. Reagan asked Fraser if they could invite the public to attend also. Fraser agreed. Dutch was elected president of the club. He was also president of the senior class by then (1928) and vice president of Boys' Hi-Y. He became art editor of the school yearbook, *The Dixonian*. He showed talent for line drawings (and also developed what became a lifelong fondness for doodling). The yearbook included both his poem "Life" and his essay "Gethsemane."

By now he had become a role model for many younger students. He himself had found surrogate fathers in the Rev. Cleaver, B. J. Fraser, and Ed Graybill. All would provide advice when asked.

Getting Ready for the Next Step

Dutch had been saving money toward college from the time he worked on the construction job. In the spring of 1928 he earned some more money as a caddy at the golf club. This was added to his lifeguard savings. Altogether, he had $400, which was not enough for a year's tuition of $180 plus living expenses.

He had his eye on Eureka College. His inspiration was Garland Waggoner, the son of the late minister of the Disciples of Christ (who had died shortly before the Reagan boys were baptized). Six years earlier, Garland had been the fullback, captain, and star of Dixon's football team. He went on to Eureka, where he was also a star player.

Eureka was a Disciples of Christ school, located some one hundred miles south of Dixon and about twenty-five miles east of Peoria.

Dutch wanted to make the varsity football team and one day equal Garland's success, despite his nearsightedness. Football helmets didn't have metal face guards in those days, so it was difficult to wear glasses on the field, but Dutch could succeed as a lineman, where distance vision was not a necessity. He had his self-confidence and was sure that would get him through.

Margaret had her father's blessing to attend Eureka. Her eldest sister was a Eureka graduate, and her sister Helen was already a student there. Margaret saw Eureka as the start of a journey that would take her to many parts of the world. She was trim, pretty, vivacious, poised, and had a good sense of humor.

Although Dutch did not have the funds to enroll, he did have an appointment with Eureka's Dean Samuel Harrod and a place to stay for one night. So, one September day, with Margaret's car piled with her possessions, he joined her for the auto trip to Eureka. As they left town, they passed the big Chautauqua shed where he had spoken at their graduation (he had quoted from the New Testament, John 10:10: "I have come in order that they have life in all its abundance").

For Ronald Reagan, one important chapter in his life was coming to end, although Dixon would be "home" for several more years. He greatly liked its feeling of being a small-town "family." As he wrote years later, "All of us have to have a place we go back to; Dixon is that place for me."[6]

Chapter Eight

Eureka College

"I fell head over heels in love with Eureka. . . . It seemed to me then, as I walked up the path, to be another home," Ronald Reagan wrote in his memoir thirty-seven years later.[1] It is true that he immediately felt he had found the perfect fit for him. And why? It was partly because the leafy campus marked the beginning of a new era in his life; partly because he liked adventure and this would be one; partly because it was located in another comfortably sized town; partly because Margaret was there; and partly because hardly anyone there knew that he was the son of a "town drunk," as many did in Dixon.

Sturdy Pioneers

Eureka was (and still is) a small liberal arts college (250 students when Reagan attended; nearly 800 today). It received its charter from the state of Illinois on February 6, 1855. Its founders, led by Ben Major, were ardent abolitionists.

Major was a successful Kentucky farmer who wanted to liberate the slaves he had inherited from his father. To prepare them for freedom, he gradually taught them to read and write. In 1831, leaving his family behind and his slaves caring for the farm, he left on horseback in search of congenial new land. He got as far as Walnut Grove, Illinois, on the banks of a lively creek. It was a small settlement about twenty-five miles east of the present-day city of Peoria. Its leaders proposed that all followers of Jesus Christ free themselves from the divisions caused by denominational creeds in order to foster a community spirit. This appealed to Major.

He returned to Kentucky to make arrangements to take his slaves to New York City and thence by ship to the new country of Liberia, in Africa, to become settlers. In 1835 he and his family set out for Walnut Grove and settled there. They first built a log cabin, then a family home in which they schooled their children.

By 1848 the settlement had nearly forty young children needing schooling. Major wrote to a nephew, asking if he could recommend a teacher for a school they wanted to build. The nephew recommended Asa Starbuck Fisher, a young teacher from Galesburg who had attended the Knox Manual Labor Institute there. He was hired.

As the school year came to an end, the town fathers were pleased with Fisher's work and asked him to stay, for they were going to raise the money to build a schoolhouse—which they did. It was first called Walnut Grove Seminary. In 1850 they changed the name to Walnut Grove Academy. Its curriculum was based on the inclusive Christian outlook and community spirit that had drawn Ben Major to the community.

One day that spring, Major and Fisher were walking toward the edge of the settlement when Major turned and pointed to a hillock opposite and announced that he was speaking for the elders of the community and they planned to build a college on that site. They wanted Fisher to be its president. When the time came for that plan to become a reality, Fisher accepted the offer.

Local Eureka legend has it that, right after felling the first tree on what would become the college site, Major drove his ax into the stump and declared, "Here we'll build our school."

The elders of Walnut Grove applied to Washington, D.C., for a post office in that name. They were turned down because there was already a Walnut Grove some ninety miles to the west. They then hit upon the name "Eureka" for their post office, their settlement, and their college.

Major died in 1853 before work on the first college buildings could be completed. The Academy continued on until February 6, 1855, when it received its state charter as Eureka College.

From the beginning, the college kept tuition as low as possible and aided many students whose families were poor. As a Disciples of Christ school, Eureka eschewed denominational teaching, but it did encourage students to regularly study their Bibles and attend chapel. To this day, Eureka College is affiliated with the Christian Church (Disciples of Christ). Religion to the college was a matter of teaching values. Its catalog published four years after Reagan's graduation read, "Religious values shall be found in courses of study . . . and in recreational activities. The development of religious attitudes is essential."

It was the first coeducational college in Illinois and only the third in the nation. Having both young men and women enrolled and attending classes together fit the founders' religious tenets that all people were created equal. There would be no discrimination of any kind at Eureka College.

The town of Eureka grew up around the campus. By the time Dutch Reagan arrived, the town had approximately 1,800 residents (in the year 2000 the population was 4,871).

What Reagan found was a campus of 112 acres, shaded by tall elms. It had five main buildings arranged in a semicircle. The stately 1870s administration building was in the center (and still performs its initial purposes today). The buildings were made of brick and influenced by English Georgian architecture. (Since Reagan's days at Eureka there have been several new buildings added. They are contemporary in design but also built of brick and blend in comfortably with the old ones.)

"Eureka" is from an ancient Greek word meaning "I have found it"—and that describes exactly Reagan's reaction to the college. (Coincidentally, it is also the state motto of California.)

Getting In

On arriving at the campus, Reagan's first objective, after helping Margaret get installed, was to get himself enrolled. Thanks to the boyfriend of Margaret's sister, he had been invited to bunk the first night at the Tau Kappa Epsilon ("Teke") house, one of three national Greek letter fraternities on campus.

The next morning he had his meeting with Dean Samuel Harrod, who was also the college registrar. Harrod was a professor of classics, with a Princeton education. He listened sympathetically, since Eureka attracted many students who needed financial assistance.

The school was struggling at that time. The farm economy of Illinois was sagging, and the school depended upon the various Disciples of Christ churches in Illinois for most of its annual budget of more than $600,000. Those churches, like the farm families that supported them, were also feeling the tight times. Reagan quickly learned, as he put it later, "We had a special spirit at Eureka that bound us all together, much as a poverty-stricken family is bound."[2]

While Reagan had satisfactory grades in high school, they weren't high enough to merit an academic scholarship, so Dean Harrod introduced him to the football coach and athletic director, Ralph "Mac" McKinzie. Reagan, mindful that Garland Waggoner from Dixon had been Eureka's most recent star, embroidered his own accomplishments on the Dixon team. McKinzie was used to young players puffing up their records, but he liked the young man's enthusiasm and determination (and was also impressed by his swimming experience), so agreed on an athletic scholarship of $90, which would pay for half his tuition.

The $400 in savings that Dutch had brought with him to Eureka would be apportioned as follows: $90 for tuition, $270 for his room at the fraternity house, $5 for an enrollment fee, and $35 for spending money that had to last from September until the following May! He was given a job to cover his board: washing dishes at the Teke house. In his second year he "graduated" to a job "cleansing tableware" at a girls' dormitory. For his junior and senior years he earned his board money as the college's swimming pool lifeguard and official swimming coach.

His course schedule that first year included English literature, zoology, history, and rhetoric; in addition there was physical education, football, and swimming.

No Flaming Youth Here

This was toward the end of the "flaming youth" craze that had swept the nation. It was a case of youthful rebellion without political or radical motivation. Raccoon coats, bootleg liquor, party crashing, and very short skirts and bobbed hair on girls were all part of it. Not, however, on the Eureka campus. Most of the students were from rural Illinois, most were members of the Disciples of Christ (although no more than 20 percent were studying for the ministry), and they were conventional in their social behavior.

Eureka's students did want the college to lift its ban on dancing. Until 1928 there was an annual event, called "the Grind," in which an orchestra played and circles of boys and girls moved in opposite directions. Each time the music stopped, the students would introduce themselves to the counterpart they were facing. After a time, the music would stop altogether, and the students had ice cream and cookies. Even this tame event was banned by Eureka's president, Bert Wilson. The college was deeply in debt; Wilson was applying for a grant from the large Disciples of Christ organization, and he believed this showing of puritanical zeal would appeal to its trustees. (The Disciples of Christ church did not approve of dancing.)

Wilson had not fully considered the student reaction to his ban. Upon learning of it, the several fraternities and sororities organized off-campus dinners, followed surreptitiously by dancing. There was also the Legion Hall in town. Student groups took to using it and, of course, dancing.

One night, one of the students, hiding behind a bush as the others entered, wrote down the names of those attending and turned them in to the president's office.

All that the students were asking was for the tight ban to be relaxed somewhat. Instead, what they got from Wilson were more restrictions and extra work for those whose names had been turned in. This was a mistake. Farm aid had been reduced, hurting many local families. There were few jobs for new graduates. Eighty students had recently dropped out for economic reasons.

As he later remarked many times, Dutch did not feel poor, because everyone else seemed to be in the same boat. This situation increased what was called "the Eureka Spirit"—helping out one another, the absence of snobbery, and a willingness to sacrifice personally for the good of the whole group.

Football

Ralph McKinzie had taken on the job of athletic director and football coach during his own senior year at Eureka. Born in Oklahoma, "Mac" was not yet thirty when Dutch Reagan began at Eureka.

In his undergraduate days, Mac had been an all-conference fullback for four years and all-conference guard on the basketball team. Eureka was a member of the Little Nineteen Athletic Conference, mostly playing other small colleges, although sometimes it played much larger ones.

Tough and tenacious, Mac, in a playoff game with Bradley College, scored all fifty-two of Eureka's points. Neither tall nor large (five feet eight inches and 145 pounds), McKinzie was usually up against much larger players in football and much taller ones in basketball. This did not daunt him. He played his heart out, and both as an undergraduate and later as the athletic director and coach, he brought Eureka several glory years.

Dutch went out for football. Mac made him an end on the fifth string (he had the starting lineup and a second string of four backup squads). Reagan was puzzled and hurt by this, for he had been

Dixon's varsity end. He began to believe that the coach disliked him. The reason he never saw play that season was that McKinzie realized his nearsightedness made it difficult for him to see the ball carrier. Mac also had larger, more talented players to put in. Nevertheless, McKinzie liked Reagan's energy and determination. Dutch came out for every practice and did every exercise without complaining. McKinzie was a tough taskmaster, but he appreciated Reagan's ability to remember every play he had been taught in practices.

About Reagan's first season, Eureka's yearbook for 1928–29 noted, "He has the determination and fight which will finally win out if he sticks to football throughout his college career."

Mac thought Reagan was cut out to be a swimming standout, but he understood the young man had his heart set on being a football star, so he encouraged Dutch to keep coming out for football. Dutch did indeed excel at swimming. That freshman year he won every event he entered—the crawl, the backstroke, and both the 100-meter and 200-meter relays. In both sports, Dutch's warm personality made him many friends. McKinzie commented, "Other kids on the squad came to me to speak for him . . . and I knew he didn't put them up to it. He was a leader and used his power well."[3]

The Dramatic Club

Dutch also joined the Dramatic Club, whose adviser was Miss Ellen Johnson. He yearned to get back into acting, but Margaret's interest in the club was at least as important a reason for him to join.

Ellen Johnson had just joined the faculty as an instructor in English and French and drama coach after completing her master's degree at the University of Illinois in 1927. She was young, enthusiastic, and committed to making drama a part of student life.

Dutch was often chosen for the male lead in plays, partly because of his good looks and natural manner on the stage and partly because in those pre-microphone days, his voice carried well. He received positive reviews, which often mentioned his stage presence.

The Student Strike

The financial grant President Wilson had been seeking did not come through. As a result, he put forth a plan to the trustees to drop several courses and terminate the faculty members teaching them. Some of these were courses needed by seniors and juniors to meet graduation requirements, so anxiety among them was sharp, as was faculty opposition to the plan. Rumors had it that Wilson would next propose dropping sports. It was well known that Wilson thought competitive and league sports were incompatible with the mission of a religious school.

The students' unhappiness with Wilson's crackdown on dancing now merged with anger over his plan. He had not consulted faculty or students on any of his moves to this point, and this failure increased anxieties and opposition.

On Friday, November 16, Wilson addressed an open meeting in the chapel. He criticized sharply the morals of the student body and the town. He painted a gloomy picture of Eureka's future. As a result, town sentiment now turned against him, as had faculty and students already. He submitted a letter of resignation to the board of trustees.

Eureka's football season finale with Illinois College was to be played on Saturday, the seventeenth. Scheduled for that evening was a meeting of the trustees to take up Wilson's plan and his letter of resignation. Wilson's opposition felt sure the trustees would neither accept his resignation nor turn down his "consolidation" plan (the name he gave it).

The next week, a group of alumni issued a statement calling on the trustees to accept the resignation, even though they had not as yet. The student newspaper, *Pegasus*, supported their call. Criticism of Wilson focused on the statement in his speech that Eureka was "confronted with a dark future." Students discussed among themselves the idea of leaving at the end of the semester and not returning.

This idea did not gel; however, restlessness pervaded the campus for the entire week. On Tuesday, the twentieth, the board's president received a petition signed by 145 students (nearly two-thirds of the student body) asking for Wilson's resignation. Two days later, the board's executive committee met with a delegation of twenty-one students.

A week later, on Tuesday the twenty-seventh, the trustees met for most of the day and well into the evening to discuss the problems. They did not accept Wilson's resignation, and they did accept his "consolidation" plan to save money, even expanding it to reduce to eight the number of teaching departments, one fewer than Wilson had proposed. The student petition to accept Wilson's resignation was rejected.

Fury at this decision was centered at Reagan's Teke house. Les Pierce, the chapter's president and a first-string player on the Golden Tornadoes, the football team, took the lead in denouncing Wilson as having "sold out" the students.

Most students had been expected to leave for home after classes that day for the Thanksgiving holiday, but with the trustees' meeting outcome not yet known, nearly all were still on campus. Pierce and several others went to the other fraternities and sororities, the dormitories and faculty houses. Then, at 11:45 p.m., they rang the chapel bell nonstop for fifteen minutes. People came running, some in nightclothes covered by their overcoats. The chapel was soon packed. Pierce presided.

Earlier, when Pierce and the other leaders laid the plan for the meeting, they had decided that the speech that would call everyone to action should be delivered by a freshman who would be on campus for four years. It was thought that a senior might be accused of self-interest, since his or her classes would be directly affected.

Once that decision was made, attention turned to Dutch Reagan. His good voice and platform "presence" would be just right for the occasion. They reviewed with him the points to be made.

Before he took the floor there was intense, heated discussion. At one point a Eureka music teacher who was present led the crowd in singing spirituals.

Finally, it was Dutch's moment to speak. He wrote later, "I'd been told I should sell the idea so there'd be no doubt of the outcome."[4] He later wrote, "For the first time in my life, I felt my words reach out and grab an audience, and it was exhilarating." When the time came for him to put forward the planned motion to call for a student strike, "everybody rose to their feet with a thunderous clapping of hands and approved the proposal . . . by acclamation."[5]

The statement the students voted for declared that they were going on strike immediately, "pending the acceptance of President Wilson's resignation by the board of trustees." The president of the student body and another student took a copy of that statement, with the notation that the students would stay out on strike until Wilson's resignation, and slipped it under his door.

The next day the students went home for Thanksgiving. Heavy clouds hung over northwestern Illinois, and it turned to heavy rain that evening. Back home, Dutch found the family was having money trouble, and there was strain between Jack and Nelle. He offered to return home to help out after the current semester ended. Nelle would not hear of it.

The following Monday, back on campus, Dutch found snow replacing the rain. The strike was under way. Only six students went to class, and two of them were Wilson's daughters.

Reporters swarmed over the campus. On Thursday, December 6, United Press ran a dispatch based on a rumor to the effect that the college would be moved to Springfield. There was no truth in it.

The trustees met again on the seventh. This time, Wilson's resignation was accepted.

None of the classes Wilson had wanted to drop were dropped. Also, dances were to become a part of campus life. In fact, to celebrate their victory, the students immediately held one on campus.

Ending the Freshman Year

Ronald Reagan's goal was not to become a great student, just a good enough one to pass muster. He relied on his superb memory and his gift for language to get him comfortably through English, history, and rhetoric. Later, when he took economics courses, he readily understood the logic underlying the stated principles. Margaret thought he could be an excellent student if he just put more effort into studying. He was, however, satisfied with his own priorities, and the first ones were sports, drama, and, now, politics. Some years later, he told an interviewer he was afraid that if his grades were too good, he would end up being an athletic teacher at a small school—and that was not his plan. His experience with the late-night speech had awakened his interest in politics. He had been part of something that had been planned and carried out successfully by students, and he had played an important role in it.

Summer 1929—Back Home

Only 8 percent of Dixon High's graduating seniors in 1928 had gone on to college, and Dutch was one of them. Most people in Dixon thought that made him a fellow to watch. In his mind, however, his first year at Eureka had been a failure in the sports department. He had not earned a letter in football (indeed, he never played in a single game), and after seeing the deftness of the basketball squad, he did not even try out for it. His heroes were stars such as Knute Rockne's "Four Horsemen" at Notre Dame, Red Grange, and Babe Ruth.

Now he was back at Lowell Park, where once again, sitting there on his lifeguard stand, he was a star. Everyone looked up to him, and the young swimmers saw him as a hero. He encouraged them, praised them, and helped give them self-confidence.

Margaret visited him often at the beach, and when the swimmers were few in number, he would take her for a ride in the beach's rowboat. Dutch would talk about his dream to one day become a professional athlete. Margaret was skeptical but did not discourage him. After all, her father, the Reverend Ben Cleaver, believed that a woman should go as far as her talents and wishes could take her, and she believed that also applied to any young man. She herself talked of foreign travel and studying other cultures. Her father, being a minister, was not wealthy, but this did not keep him or his wife, Helen, from encouraging their three daughters to make plans for their own futures.

Margaret admired Dutch's leadership qualities but was not sure he had sufficient ambition to apply them to a successful career. For his part, he was afraid that he would lose her if he couldn't return to Eureka that fall; his summer earnings at the beach would give him approximately $200 when he needed twice that, plus another scholarship. The odds looked long.

Toward the end of the summer season, opportunity knocked in the person of a land surveyor Dutch had met at the park. This man offered him a job as a rodman if he would work for a year, at the end of which the surveyor would help him get a rowing scholarship at his alma mater, the University of Wisconsin. Dutch leapt at the offer.

Two nights before it was time for Margaret to leave for Eureka, they had a date. She was unsuccessful at persuading him to try for another scholarship and a student loan. His mind was made up to the take the surveying job.

The next morning, an unexpected rainstorm pelted Dixon. It was to have been his first day on the job; however, surveyors cannot work in rain and mud, so work that day was canceled.

He remembered what his mother had often told him—that "all things are part of God's Plan, even the most disheartening setbacks and, in the end, everything worked out for the best. You stepped away from it, stepped over it, and moved on."[6]

The rainstorm he saw as one of those random events that were actually part of God's plan. He mused about football and his beloved Eureka College. Then he called Margaret to tell her he had decided he would go back to Eureka with her, after all.

His mother was thrilled. In fact, she had been promoting the idea of Neil going with him and enrolling. Moon wasn't yet persuaded, and on the morning when Dutch and Margaret were to leave, he left for work early to avoid seeing Dutch.

Eureka—the Second Year

That same day, as soon as he arrived at Eureka, everything fell into place for Ronald Reagan. He was offered a job washing dishes ("cleansing tableware," they called it) in the girls' dormitory. In addition, the college agreed to defer payment of half his tuition until after graduation. As he put it later, it was his first experience with credit.

Despite his worry that Coach McKinzie didn't like him, he immediately signed up for football again and approached the coach about Neil. He and Moon were unlike in many ways. Moon was gregarious, thought of himself as a ladies' man, enjoyed a drink, and wasn't very careful with money. Nevertheless, the brothers always supported each other when the need arose.

Dutch told the coach that while Moon had been out of high school for three years, he had been a first-rate end on the football team and was instrumental in helping the school win the county championship. He said Moon's athletic ability would be an asset to Eureka. McKinzie agreed to give Moon a partial athletic scholarship and arranged for the school to defer payment of the balance of tuition. Dutch then arranged for Moon to also get a job as a "hasher" in the kitchen of the girls' dormitory. This would cover the cost of his board at the fraternity house.

From awakening to a downpour to ending by getting his brother into his college, it had been a momentous day for Dutch. Who could blame him for thinking it all might have been part of God's plan?

When Moon came home from work at the end of that day, he found Dutch's trunk in the kitchen. He was surprised. His mother told him that Dutch had left it in the hope that Moon would change his mind about going to college.

The next morning, Moon told his boss about the incident of the trunk and that his brother had left it in order for him to put his own clothes in it and head for college. Moon thought the boss would be amused. He wasn't. About an hour later, a secretary handed him a check, but it wasn't payday. Moon asked if he was being fired. She replied that "Mr. Kennedy [the boss] says if you're not smart enough to take the good thing your brother had fixed up for you, you're not smart enough to work for him."[7]

With that, Neil Reagan left the next day for Eureka College, and the world changed for both him and for Dutch.

When they were boys, Moon, being older and bigger, was the more independent of the two. He was the leader of his group of friends in both elementary and high school. Now there was a role reversal. Ronald was already established on the small campus. He had been out for football, was in the Dramatic Club, wrote articles for *Pegasus*, and was popular. He was self-confident, self-disciplined, and had learned well the value of determination and persistence. He had the earmarks of leadership.

Moon, on the other hand, was an unknown quantity at Eureka. He was soon referred to as "Dutch Reagan's brother."

Out for Football Again

McKinzie's 1929 team was down to twenty-seven members as a result
of dropouts caused by the tough economic times. Nevertheless, initially he put Moon on the second squad. He knew Moon was varsity
material, "fast, quick-eyed, tough to avoid . . . [but] I held him back
so he could season."[8]

Dutch meanwhile had bestowed his fraternity pin on Margaret
(this was widely interpreted to mean they were "engaged to be
engaged"). His next goal was actually to play on the football team.

Instead, McKinzie relegated him this time not to the fifth squad
(because there were no longer enough players to make up five squads),
but to what might be called the second-and-a-half squad.

His attitude toward the coach was "I'll show him." He was determined to get Mac's attention by blocking and tackling as hard as he
possibly could during practice. One rainy practice day, they were
working on a new play. Mac told him the only way the play would
work was for the guard—Dutch—to take out the defensive halfback
before that player could stop Eureka's ball-carrying back.

Enos "Bud" Cole, who had played professional football for
three years before coming to Eureka as a sophomore, had had an
old knee injury flare up and sideline him, so he had volunteered
to serve as a coach. He took up the position of that defensive
halfback and challenged Reagan to block him. "Never before or
since did I throw such a block," Reagan recalled. "Our ex-officio
coach ascended . . . and seemed to dangle in the air before plum-

meting to the ground. As I returned to the huddle, he limped off the field."[9]

After the practice, Dutch and a fellow player were walking back to the fraternity house when they noticed Coach McKinzie walking behind them. He didn't usually go home that way. He caught up to them and said to Dutch, "You're doing fine. Keep it up."[10] The next Saturday, Dutch was in the starting lineup and played the remaining games of that season and the next two.

Decades later, McKinzie told a *Chicago Sun-Times* reporter, "He [Reagan] was not a star by any means, but he was a good, conscientious, dedicated player—enthusiastic about sports, which he lived for. He was good in dramatics, too. After a game he used to imitate an announcer [using a broomstick as a microphone] and recount the plays. He had us all in stitches."[11]

The college's yearbook, *The Prism*, for 1929–30, summarized Reagan's playing season: "Reagan advanced from last year's second squad to the first team this year. He never gives up when the odds are against him. Dutch made his letter easily this season and should be a mainstay next year."

Chapter Nine

Eureka College— the Depression Years

The great market crash of October 1929 had not made things notably worse for Eureka College or its students, mainly because things were bad already. Now that he was in college, Moon no longer had money to send home to their parents, but they managed somehow. Dutch, in addition to his girls' dormitory job, picked up some change by helping Henry "Heinie" Brubaker, the college's engineer and bell ringer (he rang the chapel bell at the beginning and end of every class period). Dutch raked leaves, mowed lawns, and in winter thawed water pipes. The small amounts he earned were not enough to send home.

He and Margaret went to several dances together and acted in a number of plays put on by Epsilon Sigma, the college's drama club that dramatic coach Ellen Johnson had formed.

Back home in Dixon that summer, both Reagan brothers were at work—a situation not matched by some of their former high school classmates who had not found work since graduating. Moon got a job with a construction company, and Dutch was back at his lifeguard stand on the Lowell Park beach. Margaret seemed to Dutch more beautiful than ever with her dark eyes and hair, her ready laugh and assured manner. They went to the movies often, seeing the Marx Brothers, Greta Garbo, and Jean Harlow, among other stars of the day. Afterward they would go to the local soda fountain for cherry phosphates. It was a happy summer for him. He was cutting more lifesaver notches in the old log, and the usual band of young admirers flocked around his lifeguard stand.

Things were not so happy, however, for Nelle and Jack. Not only were there fewer commissions from sales at the Fashion Boot Shop to be applied to Jack's half interest, but his base pay was also less. They moved into a smaller place.

At the end of summer, Margaret had a surprise for Dutch that was not a happy one. She announced that she would take her junior year at the University of Illinois in Champaign. She said she wanted to acquire broader knowledge than she could from the courses at Eureka College and tried to soften the news by reminding him that Champaign was closer than Dixon was to Eureka. Thus they would see each other often in Eureka, and between times she would write often. Dutch was not happy, of course, but knew better than to try to get his self-sufficient sweetheart to change her mind. They said farewell on the Eureka campus the day he returned for his junior year.

Margaret's mother, Helen, may have been the inspiration for her taking her junior year away from Eureka. Although she liked Dutch, considering the mores of the time she probably would have been concerned about Reagan's father being an alcoholic and a Catholic. In any case, she probably thought a "cooling off" period would be a good idea.

Junior Year

With Margaret absent, Dutch threw himself into school activities with increased intensity. He became president of the Boosters' Club, basketball team cheerleader, one of the editors of the yearbook, a member of the student senate, treasurer of the drama society, and official coach of the swimming team. He also continued his acting and his football. In spring he earned his second varsity letter on the track team.

Room at the Reagan "Inn"

For an away football game that season, the team was to stop in Dixon on the way and spend the night. Dutch was to stay with the rest of the team.

At that time, a close of friend of Reagan's, William Franklin "Burgie" Burghardt, was one of two African American players on the team (after college days he chaired several university chemistry departments). The other was Jim Rattan.

While the bus waited, Mac went into the hotel in Dixon to arrange for the rooms. After what seemed like an unusually long time, Dutch went in to find out what was causing the delay. Mac told him the hotel would not take their two black players. McKinzie said they would go someplace else, but the manager had said no hotel in Dixon would take "colored boys." In that case, Mac said, they would all sleep on the bus.

Dutch had an alternative suggestion. If Mac did that, the two black teammates would be upset that they had inconvenienced the entire team. Instead, he suggested that Mac tell everyone there weren't enough rooms for the entire team and that three of them—Burgie, Rattan, and Dutch—would go to the Reagan home for the night. Mac was skeptical that the Reagan parents would like the idea. Dutch knew better. Indeed, when the three of them showed up at the door, Reagan later recalled, Nelle said, "'Well, come on in,' her eyes brightening with a warmth felt by all three of us."[9] Nelle and Jack were color-blind when it came to race, and they saw these teammates as just two more of Dutch's friends.

Onstage

Of all the fourteen stage productions in which Ronald Reagan appeared during his college years, the one that had the greatest effect on him was Edna St. Vincent Millay's *Aria Da Capo*, a one-act play with a pacifist theme. It was set in ancient Greece. He played the Shepherd who was strangled just before the final curtain.

Reagan's interest in the stage probably originated with his many appearances with Nelle in her Bible-based skits and dramatic readings. Then, in his freshman year of college, the Cleavers had taken Dutch and Margaret to see a touring company production of the play *Journey's End*, a World War I tragedy that centered on the battered emotions of one Captain Stanhope. Reagan later wrote, "I was drawn to the stage that night as if it were a magnet."[2] (In the summer of 1930, Dutch and Margaret saw a film version of the play at the Dixon Theater.)

Ellen Johnson, the new English professor on the Eureka faculty, loved teaching dramatics and coaching young players. "Theater arts" was an extracurricular activity at that time. Johnson increased the number of student productions, and Dutch and Margaret began trying out for many of them. One play was *Journey's End*, and Dutch, to his delight, found himself cast as Captain Stanhope. Johnson also created the Dramatic Club, which gave students interested in the theater opportunities to work together year round rather than just for the rehearsal period before a new play was to be staged.

Even before staging *Aria Da Capo*, Johnson had sufficient confidence in her young players that she entered Eureka into a prestigious one-act-play contest at Northwestern University. Well-known universities and colleges from all over the country were entered in this annual contest. Eureka was undoubtedly the smallest and the only one without a full-time dramatic arts department. Eureka won second place in the competition, and Reagan was one of three actors singled out for individual awards. Afterward, the head of Northwestern's speech department, which had sponsored the competition, asked him if he had thought about making acting his career. He said he had not. The professor then said, "Well, you should."

During his junior year, Dutch played the lead in four productions. Toward the end of the school year he had the role of the playboy brother of a stuffy, domineering man who saves a young woman from his brother's lust. The play, *The Brat*, was loosely based on George Bernard Shaw's *Pygmalion*, with the young woman being the Eliza Doolittle equivalent. With Margaret away, Reagan became infatuated with the leading lady, who was older than her fellow players. He called it the "disease" of "leadingladyitis." Then Margaret returned home, as cheerful and attractive as ever, and he was immediately "cured" of the "disease." The best news from Margaret was that she would return to Eureka College for their senior year.

Summer of 1931

Dutch was back at the lifeguard stand at Lowell Park, happy to have his job again and with no reduction in salary. The Depression had not spared Dixon. Several factories had closed, farms were being foreclosed, the price of milk was way down—hitting the local dairies hard. Like just about everything else, the Dixon market for shoes—let alone fashionable, expensive ones—had also dried up. At the end of summer and after eight years of Jack Reagan's being on the job, the nearly elegant Fashion Boot Shop closed its doors for good. With it went Jack's earlier dream of one day owning half the shop. Now he took a job as a traveling shoe salesman, but his modest twenty-two-dollars-a-week salary had to cover his expenses as well. Nelle was able to get a job as a seamstress at a women's clothing shop. She tackled the job with her usual determination and energy. She waited on customers, fitted them, altered, sold, and pressed garments, and cleaned up the shop at the end of the day, never complaining about the hours or the workload.

Senior Year

Early in the fall, the Reverend Ben Cleaver received the "call" by the Disciples of Christ Church in Eureka to become its minister. Meanwhile, Dutch was elected president of the senior class at school. Jack had lost his traveling job but was able to get a job managing a small, cut-rate shoe store in Springfield, the state capital—but it was about 80 miles south of Eureka and 150 miles south of Dixon. For the next three months Jack and Nelle were separated while he roomed in Springfield, for he could not afford the gasoline to drive home.

On September 24, on his way south to Springfield to begin the new job, Jack stopped at Eureka College to visit his sons and spent the night at the Teke fraternity house.

After that, Dutch and Moon visited Jack once when their football team went to Springfield for a game. One of them described the shoe store as a "hole-in-the-wall" and garish—quite a comedown from the Fashion Boot Shop.

On that trip, the boys were able to take Jack back to the college dormitory where they were spending the night and have him join the team for dinner. Despite his miserable job, Jack was in top storytelling form. He regaled the team and Coach McKinzie with nonstop stories.

Dutch's Major

In 1927, Eureka's one-man economics department, Professor Alexander Charles Gray, introduced a hybrid major, economics-sociology. Since economics dealt with money, sociology dealt with people, and money affects people, the melding seemed logical to him.

A. C. Gray had come to Eureka in 1908 after earning his bachelor's degree at the University of Toronto and his master's at Ohio's Hiram College. He was also an ordained Disciples of Christ minister, deeply interested in Christian social theory. This led to his interest in populism. Nevertheless, he used a then-traditional textbook, *The History of Economic Thought: A Critical Account of the Origin and Development of Economic Theories of the Leading Thinkers in the Leading Nations*, by Lewis H. Haney (first published in 1911). Haney, by coincidence, was a native of Eureka.

As a teacher, Gray was an iconoclast. At one point, he recommended that Reagan read a biography of Lenin (Gray was also college librarian at the time). Some years later, Gray invited the socialist Norman Thomas, who ran for president several times, to come to the campus to address the students. Some eight hundred attended the lecture.

In later years, Reagan became a devoted reader of the works of economists Frédéric Bastiat, Friedrich Hayek, and Milton

Friedman, but as an undergraduate he more or less breezed through his courses. He accumulated Bs, some Cs, but three D grades. He did not do much studying, relying on his excellent memory. (In his address at the dedication of the campus's Melick Library in 1967, Reagan quipped, "Ten years ago I was just across the campus there to receive an honorary degree. As I told some of you at that time, I had always figured the first degree you gave me was honorary.")

Brother Neil said Professor Gray, known as a lenient grader (his students called him "Daddy Gray"), complained that Dutch scarcely opened a book, yet "when the test comes, I just have to give him his grade." Moon contended his brother had a photographic memory: "He would take a book the night before the test . . . in about an hour he would thumb through it and 'photograph' those pages and write a good test."[3]

Dutch had signed up for the dual major because, as he once put it, he figured he would be in a business where he had to deal with money. Professor Gray wanted his students to understand the uses and work of money in an economy, but he also emphasized to them the plight of modern workers in such places as coal mines and automobile factories. His purpose was to increase the social awareness of his students and build their interest in reform.

Another faculty member, geology professor Jake Rinker, later recalled in an interview, "Ronald was an extrovert, popular with everybody. He didn't really stand out academically, but he was popular from the start and a better-than-average student."[4]

Jack's Christmas "present"

On Christmas Eve, Jack was home and the family was together in the small Dixon apartment that Jack and Nelle now occupied. Nelle improvised decorations, and she and Jack had small, inexpensive presents for each other and one each for Dutch and Moon. Just as the boys were about to leave to pick up their dates, a special-delivery envelope for Jack arrived. He opened it as the others stood around. Jack thought the blue envelope might contain a Christmas bonus. Instead, after he read it, he said in a soft but bitter voice, "Well, it's a hell of a Christmas present. I've been laid off."

After the holidays, Jack and Nelle moved into one of the two bedrooms and rented the other. A hot plate in the bedroom became their kitchen. The grocer cut off their credit. Neighbors sent food trays over to them. Dutch sent all he could afford from his dishwashing job—fifty dollars.

The Depression deepened in Eureka, Dixon—nearly everywhere. Nevertheless, as Reagan later wrote, "There was a spirit of warmth and helpfulness and, yes, kindliness abroad in the land that was inspiring to me as we all clung to the belief that, sooner or later, things would get better."[5]

Jack—with no job now—threw himself into volunteer work at the Democratic Party headquarters. He was an ardent Democrat and was convinced that if they could defeat Hoover they would bring an end to the Depression.

The school's finances were in perilous shape. It cut costs wherever possible. That year's yearbook was one victim. Football team trips to distant towns were impossible; the money for travel was not there. Mac McKinzie used all his persuasive powers to get opposing teams to come to Eureka to play.

Catherine McKeever Spayer, who was in Dutch's class, performed in several plays with him. After classes she often went to Haecker's Restaurant, where her mother, Fern, was the cook. In those days, if he could afford it, Dutch would go to the restaurant after sports practice. She later recalled these incidents: "He could come in the restaurant about 10 minutes to 7 p.m., when Mom had the grill turned off and the kitchen cleaned up for the night. She would surprise Dutch with a steak, since she knew he couldn't afford one. He usually ordered hamburgers."[6]

In a letter to Mrs. Spayer years later, Reagan wrote, "I'll never forget your mother. I never knew how much trouble I caused with my late orders."

Catherine Spayer said he always remembered to help clean up the kitchen after one of these late meals. One winter day he was paid one dollar to crawl under the building to thaw out the frozen water pipes.

Graduation Day

By graduation day, June 7, 1932, the senior class was down to forty-five students. Many had dropped out to save their families the money, others to help out at home or on the farm.

Despite the economic gloom on everyone's mind, the graduating seniors had a clear and beautiful day for their ceremony. The smell of freshly mowed grass was in the air.

The Reverend Cleaver, in a prayer to bless the students, asked that they "hold God and God's word in their hearts." As class president, Dutch spoke to the assemblage. So did the new college president, Clyde Lyon. Lyon's purpose was to inspire them to see beyond the dark days of the present to a brighter future. He urged the new graduates not to let the immediate prospect of a dark future "bully them into non-achievements."

In addition to receiving their diplomas, the students had a special three-decade-old tradition to carry out. All forty-five stood in a circle. They held a "rope" of ivy cut down from the brick walls of one of the college's buildings. Each was to break the section of ivy he or she held, symbolizing a break with the past and a move into the future. The exceptions were those couples standing side by side who intended to stay "connected" to each other. They were not to break the part of the ivy between them. Margaret and Dutch were one of the couples who continued to hold the ivy.

All sang the college's alma mater, "'Neath the Elms," then let out a lusty cheer and said their goodbyes to college life and one another.

Chapter Ten

The Search for a Job

Back home in Dixon after graduation, Dutch had his lifeguard job once again, and Moon had been rehired by the cement company, but on a reduced salary. Dutch was able to put ten dollars a week toward the family's budget from his job.

Jack was fired up over the prospect of Franklin D. Roosevelt becoming president and worked full time as a volunteer at the Dixon Democratic office (the Democratic National Convention was in Chicago that summer). Without an income from him, their budget rested mostly on Nelle's salary at the dress shop.

Jack managed to keep his used Oldsmobile, just in case a new traveling job turned up. They had moved once again, to a two-room apartment 207 North Galena Street. Thus, Neil and Ronald would have a bedroom of their own.

Many people were worse off than the Reagans. On June 7, the day of Dutch's graduation, twenty-five thousand World War I veterans gathered in Washington and marched up Pennsylvania Avenue toward the U.S. Capitol to demand early payment of the bonus certificates the government had granted them for their war service. Most carried homemade signs with such declarations as "Wilson's Heroes, Hoover's Bums."

The House of Representatives passed a bill granting the early payment, but the Senate turned it down. Some veterans returned home dejected, but thousands stayed, occupying empty buildings on Pennsylvania Avenue and a camp they had set up across the Anacostia River, but still inside the District of Columbia.

On July 28, D.C. police tried to evict the bonus marchers. A riot ensued, and two of the veterans were killed by police fire. Local authorities appealed to President Hoover for help. He ordered General Douglas MacArthur to use federal troops to break up the encampments. The troops succeeded in ousting the veterans from the Pennsylvania Avenue buildings, then went to Anacostia to drive the rest out with tear gas, after which they torched their improvised shelters.

It didn't take long for the outrage to spill across the country, including Dixon. Democrats especially were incensed. Both Jack and Ronald deplored what they thought was excessive force being used against a defenseless group that had a reasonable request.

Meanwhile, Congress adjourned in July after passing a very weak farm aid bill, which would provide a family of four an average of fifty cents a day. Many local dairy, corn, and wheat farms were being foreclosed.

That summer a Chicago evangelist, Paul Rader, launched what he called a "Pantry of Plenty" system to help feed poor families. In Dixon, the Disciples of Christ Church and eighteen others churches joined the plan. Canning experts arrived with equipment, and the local drive took in donations of fresh fruit and vegetables, as well as meat and poultry. Over eight weeks, the experts canned everything. They left with 5,891 cans to distribute in Chicago, with an equal number remaining to feed Dixon's own needy citizens.

The Walgreen "Castle"

Charles Walgreen, the founder of the drugstore chain, a local native, long had it in mind that when he was prosperous he would have a country place. When he became a millionaire several times over, he and his wife, Myrtle, bought Hazelwood, the once-grand 1870s estate on the Rock River that had fallen into ruin after the manor house burned down. At first, the Walgreens built a log cabin as their retreat. Then, in 1932, they developed the property into a great estate. The main house had a reception room with one wall entirely of windows—120 feet long and 40 feet high—to take in the view. The house had a pool room, a wine cellar, and a tunnel to the original log cabin, which became a guest cottage.

Hazelwood acquired a swimming pool, stables, and riding trails. People in Dixon called it "the castle on the hill." Did the people of Dixon resent this rich couple spending so much money on a lavish estate? No. On the contrary, it gave them a feeling of importance, that this successful businessman and his wife had chosen their city for their country home. Not only that—it provided many jobs during construction, plus work for caterers and others at the Walgreens' many large parties. The grounds required maintenance. The house needed a staff. It also told Dutch Reagan and his friends and neighbors that the American Dream was still alive: hard work, persistence, and answering when opportunity knocked could still produce great success.

Dutch was hoping one of those opportunities would present itself to him through the auspices of one of Lowell Park's summer residents. Sid Altschuler was a prosperous Kansas City businessman. He and his wife, Helen, and their two daughters had taken one of the Lowell Park cottages for the summer. Dutch had taught their daughters to swim. Altschuler liked this engaging young man. One day, they were sitting on the beach watching the Altschuler girls demonstrate their newfound aquatic talents when Sid asked Dutch what he wanted to do when the summer was over. Dutch didn't know and said so.

Altschuler suggested he think it over for a few days, then let him know. He said that if it was in a field where he had connections, he would do everything he could to open doors for Reagan.

Dutch did think it over—intensively. He was enough of a realist by now to know that he was not going to have a career in professional football. Swimming offered no career opportunities (and lifeguarding was not a career). His secret ambition was to go into acting professionally, but even suggesting it would no doubt make Mr. Altschuler think he had taken leave of his senses.

Gradually, his thoughts turned to radio. It was a rapidly growing medium. He had a fine voice, well modulated, clear, resonant. Sports were being broadcast more and more, and there were already a few renowned sportscasters. That was it! He would tell Mr. Altschuler that he wanted to be a radio sports announcer.

He did. Altschuler thought it was a promising choice; however, it was a field in which he had no contacts. Although this was a disappointment, it was not entirely a surprise. The important thing was that Altschuler's asking of the question had caused Dutch's thoughts to crystallize into a real goal. For the rest of the summer, Dutch Reagan practiced his game-announcing routine in every spare moment, even going into his patter when he handed ice cream cones to his young swimmer customers at the snack bar.

At the Democratic Party office Jack heard from one of the volunteers that there was an opening in Montgomery Ward's sporting goods department. Dutch lost no time in going to the store, but he was only one of several dozen applicants. With his Dixon High School sports record and his varsity letters from Eureka, he thought he stood a good chance. Instead, the job went to George Joyce, who had been a basketball star at South Dixon High, whom Dutch knew from school days.

Bearing in mind his mother's frequent advice to move on or move around any disappointment and forge ahead, he decided to do just that. The next morning Moon was going down to Eureka. Dutch would go with him, see Margaret, then hitchhike to Chicago. One of his Teke fraternity brothers was now studying medicine in Chicago, and Dutch was sure he could stay with him while he made the rounds of the big radio stations.

In Eureka, Margaret was about to begin teaching in a school not far from town. She was doubtful that Dutch's quest for a radio job would succeed. Because of the uncertainty in the air, their leave-taking was not easy.

The first driver who picked him up on the highway gave him a ride all the way to Chicago. This was a good sign, Dutch thought. It was a very hot Tuesday afternoon in September when he arrived. He went straight to the NBC building, where he was told the program director conducted interviews on Thursday.

First thing Wednesday he set off for the CBS offices, where the receptionist told him there wasn't anyone who would see him. From there he went on foot to several other stations, with no luck. He was discouraged. He set his hopes on seeing the NBC program director the next morning. There, the young receptionist informed him the program director was too busy to see anyone that day. She saw Dutch's dejection and sympathized with him. She gave him some advice. Rather than the big cities, try small ones with small stations. He would find them more willing to give a novice a chance. He thanked her and hitched his way back home to Dixon.

Jack encouraged him to follow the young woman's advice and offered to lend him the Oldsmobile. He accepted, bought gas, and set out to call on several small cities within a radius around Dixon. The farthest one was Davenport, Iowa, right across the Mississippi River, seventy miles to the west.

There his goal was WOC. The call letters stood for "World of Chiropractic," and the station was on the top floor of the Palmer School of Chiropractic Medicine. There he had no trouble getting in to see the station manager, Peter MacArthur, a Scotsman with crippling arthritis in his legs that required him to walk with two canes. MacArthur was also the station's leading announcer.

After Dutch made his pitch for a job as a sports announcer, MacArthur told him he had advertised for one for a month, interviewed ninety-four applicants, and just hired one.

Thinking the interview was over, Reagan turned to walk back to the elevator. He heard clumping and a loud voice behind him. "Not so fast, ye big bastard," MacArthur said, hitting Dutch's shin with a cane. "Do ye perhaps know football?"[1]

Dutch gave him a summary of his high school and college football experience. "Do ye think ye could tell me about a game and make me see it?" MacArthur asked. Remembering his many "broomstick broadcasts," Dutch said he could.

MacArthur led him to a studio and told him to begin when the red light on the wall went on. Reagan proceeded to re-create the fourth quarter of Eureka's game with Western State University the previous season. Eureka had been trailing 6-0, and Dutch's excitement mounted as he recounted every play and even the "chill wind" blowing across the stadium. When he was finished, MacArthur opened the door and said, "Ye did great, ye big SOB." He offered to have Reagan broadcast a game from Iowa City a week from that coming Saturday for $5 and bus fare. MacArthur added that if he did well, he could announce three more games that season. Dutch readily agreed.

When Jack heard the news, he told everyone he knew to listen to the broadcast. The plan was for Dutch to pair with a seasoned radio announcer to cover the play and the between-quarters and halftime "color." His companion had a glib radio delivery, but Dutch quickly learned his partner knew far less about football than he himself did. Dutch poured on his knowledge, and, in the third quarter, MacArthur scribbled a message to the pair, "Let the Kid finish the game." When it was over, MacArthur hired him to broadcast the next three games for $10 a game and bus fare. Dutch Reagan was now a sportscaster.

Reagan's coverage of the next games won him much praise, but as the season ended, he wondered if his new radio career was at an end. As Christmas neared, MacArthur called to offer him a regular announcer's job, starting right away, at $100 a month. That was a large salary by 1932 standards.

Dutch immediately took an $8-a-week room in Davenport, purchased weekly meal tickets at the Palmer Chiropractic School, and sent some money home to Nelle. He asked the local Disciples of Christ church minister if the Lord would consider it a tithe if he sent 10 percent to Moon each month to cover his college expenses. The minister thought the answer would be yes.

Sports events for broadcasting were few in the winter months, so Dutch found himself doing endless disc jockey announcements and reading commercials. He did not do this with the zest he put into his football broadcasts, and it was noticeable to management. After three weeks, MacArthur told him they wouldn't be needing his regular services any longer, but would call him to do sports events.

Completely deflated, Reagan went home to Dixon. Then fate stepped in. WOC called him back—temporarily—because the replacement they had hired did not work out. Dutch now found a way to put zest and his best conversational tone into the commercials and the disc announcements. MacArthur asked him to stay on permanently.

Jack Lands a Job

Not long after Franklin Roosevelt's inauguration on March 4, 1933, Jack got a job with the Works Progress Administration (WPA) managing the distribution of food to Dixon's growing number of jobless citizens. The pay was modest, but combined with Nelle's salary, they would get by.

Most of the people who lined up each day for assistance were people Jack had known for years. They were defeated and felt ashamed to be in the position of asking for handouts. What they all wanted was work, but there was virtually none. The Medusa Cement Company, where Moon had worked, had just closed, and this put nearly one thousand more Dixon people out of work.

Jack did his best to persuade a few businesses to add short-term workers, but this caused a problem. If someone got a job that lasted a few days, he went off the relief list and could not get back on for three weeks. Thus the system, perhaps unintentionally, discouraged work.

In time the WPA brought some projects to Dixon: building fences in Lowell Park, fixing the hangar at the airport, taking up the unused streetcar tracks. These and more put a number of unemployed Dixon men to work for a while.

One good byproduct of Jack's new job was that his thirst for drink diminished. He was doing something he thought was necessary and helpful to people, and despite not being able to help them as much as he wanted to, he had a sense of fulfillment.

Dutch Moves Ahead

In April 1933, MacArthur sent Reagan to Des Moines to broadcast the Drake Relays from WOC's sister station, WHO, an NBC affiliate (Drake University was a Disciples of Christ school affiliated with Eureka College). Nationally, the Drake Relays were one of the major track-and-field events of the year. For two days before the event, Dutch plunged into every detail he could find about the Relays. The result was a masterly broadcast, filled with colorful background knowledge and his communication of the excitement of the events themselves.

Shortly after Reagan returned to Davenport, "Doc" Palmer, who owned the two stations, decided to consolidate their staffs.

Most of their programming was duplicated as it was. MacArthur was moving to Des Moines and offered Dutch the job of chief sports announcer at twice his Davenport salary.

As soon as he had rented a room within walking distance of WHO, Dutch called Nelle to tell her of his good fortune. Then he called Margaret. She seemed pleased, but what was on her mind was to tell him that as soon as her current teaching assignment was over in June, she would sail to France to spend a year there with her sister Helen. Where did that leave them, he asked? "With time to find ourselves," she replied.

A year later, Margaret wrote that she had met a young U.S. consular official in France and planned to marry him. Dutch never saw her again. (Margaret was married in Richmond, Virginia, in June 1935. It was her husband's home town, and they settled there.)[2]

Chapter Eleven

The Rest of Him

Where's the Rest of Me is the title of Ronald Reagan's 1965 memoir. The title comes from a dramatic line in the film that Reagan considered to be his best, *King's Row*. In it he plays Drake McHugh, the town playboy. Drake thinks his parents left him enough money to live on indefinitely; however, a friend to whom he had given it to invest made off with it, and he is broke. So he goes to work in the railroad yard and is involved in an accident. Having passed out, he is operated on by a doctor who is the father of the girl he is interested in. When he comes to next morning, in the bedroom of Rusty, the girl from the wrong side of the tracks who has befriended him, he realizes something is very wrong—his legs are gone. He shouts to Rusty in great anguish, "Where's the rest of me?" It turns out the evil doctor amputated his legs when the injury was nowhere near that serious.

While there is a glint of a happy ending for Drake and Rusty, Reagan thought the line fit his questing for completion in his career.

When he wrote the memoir he had made his last film, the popular *General Electric Theater* had come to an end, and he was now contemplating running for governor of California. He already felt fulfilled. He had a beautiful and loving wife, children, and a satisfying sequence of careers. So, he ended the book, "I have found the rest of me." Yet there was much more to come.

From WHO to Hollywood

Soon after Dutch Reagan moved to Des Moines to work at WHO, he was broadcasting real-time re-creations of Chicago Cubs games. The plays came in by ticker tape, and the engineer in his soundproof booth would hold up cards for Reagan to read that indicated who was the batter, the pitch, whether it was a ball, strike, or hit, and the outcome of the play. Reagan would describe the action as if he were sitting in a booth above the field. Many times since, he has told the story of the time the tape stopped just as a batter came up to bat. The only thing he could do to freeze the action was have the batter foul the ball into the stands. He did this nineteen times, adding colorful details (such as kids scrambling for the ball) before the tape came back online. In reality, the batter was out on a pop fly on the first pitch thrown to him.

Dutch was the announcer for H. R. "Hal" Gross's newscasts on WHO. Gross was a Republican who, off the air, had many political discussions with Reagan. Neither changed the other's mind about party affiliation; however, Gross went on to become a several-term member of the U.S. House of Representatives, and Reagan later credited him with planting in his mind some conservative ideas.

Reagan soon became a local celebrity. WHO, as a 50,000-watt, clear-channel station, had a large and widespread audience, so that when well-known sports figures or film stars came to town, they welcomed interviews on the station. Dutch was given these assignments.

While in Des Moines his interest in horses was reawakened. A friend told him that the Fourteenth Cavalry Regiment at nearby Camp Dodge was taking on new reserve officer trainees. There he would ride excellent cavalry horses and receive equally good training in horsemanship.

He signed up. Fortunately, no eye examination was required for entry. He became an expert rider and jumper. Later, when he was in several Westerns in which he had riding scenes, he always rode them himself, rather than asking for a stuntman to substitute for him. He may have been the only film star who did his own riding on camera.

In early 1937, Dutch, still with his dream of an acting career in the back of his mind, hit upon an idea. He approached the station manager with a proposal: If he used his vacation time, would the station stake him to a trip to join the Chicago Cubs for their annual spring training on Santa Catalina Island off the Southern California coast? (Much of the island was owned by the Wrigley family, which also owned the Cubs.) There he could gather color to enliven his game coverage, get interviews with players and the manager, and otherwise turn it into a "value added" experience for WHO. The manager agreed to the plan.

On his trip with the Cubs to Catalina, he added another element. Joy Hodges, a native of Des Moines and a successful singer in Hollywood (who had also had some film roles), came home for a visit, and he interviewed her. He asked her about the possibility of acting in the movies. She said she would help him meet some useful people if he came to California. He organized his schedule to spend a few days in Hollywood at the end of his Cubs stint. She liked his enthusiasm and youthful energy and thought one of the studios might be looking for someone with his qualities. She called an agent friend, Bill Meiklejohn, and made an appointment for Dutch. Meiklejohn, upon meeting the young man, thought he had the boyish, all-American clean-cut look a studio would like. He arranged for Dutch to take a screen test at Warner Bros. the next day. He also asked him to stay in town for a few days in order to hear back from the studio. Dutch couldn't do that because he already had his train ticket to Des Moines the day after the test.

When he got to Des Moines there was a telegram awaiting him. It was from Meiklejohn: "WARNER'S OFFERS CONTRACT SEVEN YEARS, ONE YEAR'S OPTION, STARTING AT $200 A WEEK. WHAT SHALL I DO?" He immediately wired back, "SIGN BEFORE THEY CHANGE THEIR MINDS."

He was to report to the studio on June 1. In late May he broke in his replacement at WHO and packed his belongings. On his last night in Des Moines he received a rousing sendoff from his friends at their favorite roadhouse, the Moonlight Inn. The next morning he got into his new Nash convertible—his first automobile—and headed for Los Angeles.

Film Days

He was soon caught up in the ever-meshing gears of the movie business. He was liked by all who met him, and many were free with advice for this newcomer. He was happy to get it. One idea, however, he rejected: changing his name. Many stars were given new names that were thought to be more memorable, romantic, exciting, and so forth. The specialists who talked with him at the studio tried various names on him. His conclusion to them, "How about Ronald Reagan?" After some discussion they agreed. It had a natural, boy-next-door sound to it. It fit him. And that was the end of "Dutch." From then on he became known to all who met him as "Ronald," "Ron," or "Ronnie."

Within days, he was on the set for his first film, *Love Is on the Air*, in which he played a radio announcer. As usually happens with a new player, he played in "B" pictures at first. In those days theaters showed double features. One was the "A" picture with big-name stars and much publicity and advertising behind it. The "B" picture, often a few minutes shorter, had simpler production values, a mix of lesser-known and unknown players, and no publicity or advertising. "B" pictures came as part of the package of "A" movies that theater owners scheduled.

As Reagan often said of some of those early films, "They didn't necessarily want them good; they wanted them Thursday."

In time he graduated to "A" films—action Westerns, war films, comedies, romances, biographies of sport stars. He became a major film star. In all, he played in fifty-four feature-length films (this did not count the many training films he narrated or played in while he was in the Army Air Forces in World War II).

Soon after he arrived in Hollywood and knew that his first film was a certainty, he arranged to purchase a small home in Los Angeles for Jack and Nelle. In the fall of 1937 they moved from Dixon to California, where they would spend the rest of their days. Soon he began getting fan mail, and he hit upon the idea of asking Jack to coordinate its handling. It became a regular job for Jack, who took to it with gusto. He had a pass to the studio mail department and his own work area. He set up a system for logging in the fan mail, arranging for replies, and sending them with photos, if requested.

In 1939 Ronald Reagan and Jane Wyman began to date. She, too, was considered a "feature player" on contract, and her career was beginning to move. They married on January 26, 1940. Their daughter, Maureen, was born in January 1940, followed by the adoption of four-day-old Michael in March 1943.

World War II

Reagan's film career was doing well when World War II began. In March 1942 he was called up as a reserve officer, initially assigned to Fort Mason, San Francisco, which at the time was a cavalry post. This time he flunked the eye examination. This meant no overseas assignments for him. Instead he was assigned to a new Army Air Forces unit (the air force remained a part of the army until after the war). It was called the First Motion Picture Unit and was to be based at the former Hal Roach Studios in Culver City. Thus Reagan could commute from home.

The unit was made up of Hollywood professionals who dubbed their new workplace "Fort Roach." The group turned out several hundred training films during the war. Reagan narrated several and played in some. When he was discharged in 1945, he was a captain. His views on government as a fully positive force began to change during his time at Fort Roach. After dealing with many federal bureaucrats, he began to agree with his Iowa friend Hal Gross that there was plenty of waste and greed in the way federal money was spent.

Restarting His Career

Reagan was soon back in pictures, although he was becoming active in the Screen Actors Guild, which represented players in bargaining with studios for various rights. Shortly after the war ended, there began a determined effort—at first not easily detected—by Communist-inspired groups to take over certain Hollywood unions. Initially the targets were crafts unions whose members had important behind-the-scenes functions in creating movies.

Reagan began to take an active role in SAG's efforts, along with other professional groups, to stymie these takeover attempts. In 1947 he was elected SAG's president and served for three terms. It was a time when he also had ample on-the-job training in negotiations, for he went head to head with studio executives on behalf of his members. (Years later, just before his first summit meeting with Mikhail Gorbachev in 1985, he was asked if he expected to have a tough time of it. "After negotiating with those studio heads, it should be a breeze," he replied.)

During this time he also testified before the House Un-American Activities Committee in Washington about the attempted Communist takeover of Hollywood unions.

By 1948, Jane Wyman's and Ronald Reagan's film careers and interests were diverging. Her career was ascending; his was holding but not expanding. She was clearly Academy Award material and focused intensely on her work. She had no real interest in politics and thought that Ron had become obsessed about his SAG work. In 1948 they divorced. For the rest of their lives they respected each other.

New Horizons

Reagan began to date after the divorce was final. One day Mervyn LeRoy, the director, asked him to talk with a starlet, Nancy Davis, whose name had showed up on some far-left mailing lists. LeRoy thought Reagan could find a way to remedy this. They met for dinner one evening. It turned out there was another Nancy Davis in Hollywood, and it was that woman's name that was on the lists. They began dating, and on March 4, 1952, they were married. Daughter Patricia Anne ("Patti") was born October 22, 1952, and son Ronald Prescott on May 21, 1958.

By the early 1950s, Reagan was getting few good parts to consider, but his commitment to SAG work continued. At the time television was rapidly expanding its reach into the nation's homes.

Opportunity again knocked for Reagan in the form of *General Electric Theater*, which was to be a weekly live television drama. The producers wanted him to be the host and to occasionally play in it. In addition, he would travel to GE plants throughout the country, meeting with workers as they came off their shifts to talk about issues of interest to them and to showcase a well-known star. He accepted the offer. *General Electric Theater* was a highly rated success for nearly eight years, beginning in 1955. The plant tours also were very successful. His remarks to the workers reflected his growing focus on American liberty, enterprise, and problems associated with government growth.

Moon, meanwhile, had a successful career with a major advertising agency, McCann-Erickson, and managed its Los Angeles office for many years. One of his clients was the United States Borax Company, which sponsored *Death Valley Days* on television. It needed a new host, and Neil recommended his brother after the GE program ended.

By 1962 Ronald Reagan decided that the ideals expressed by Franklin Roosevelt in 1932 had not materialized in ways he said they would. The Democratic Party was moving more and more toward endless expansion of government and, he believed, reduction in individual liberty. As an actor he was in a 90 percent income tax bracket and began to question the entire taxing-and-spending structure of the federal government.

That was when he changed his registration to Republican. He explained it this way, "I didn't leave the Democratic Party; it left me."

In 1964 he not only supported his friend Barry Goldwater's candidacy for president, but also recorded a late-campaign television speech that had two electrifying effects: it immediately raised over $1 million for the Goldwater campaign, and it made Reagan a national political figure.

Running for Governor

In 1965, friends persuaded Reagan to "explore" a 1966 campaign against California governor Edmund G. "Pat" Brown, who would be running for a third term. Reagan went on to win a Republican primary election, then defeated Brown by nearly one million votes.

He was reelected for a second term in 1970. Over eight years he returned a portion of budget surpluses to taxpayers, dealt with student unrest at the University of California (Berkeley), saved Indian ranches from a large federal dam (Round Valley), and negotiated substantial reforms of the welfare system with a legislature controlled by the Democrats.

He left office with strong approval ratings and, as a private citizen, embarked on a busy schedule involving speaking engagements, a daily radio commentary, and a syndicated newspaper column.

The 1976 Presidential Nomination

Reagan wanted to give Gerald Ford, the new president after Richard Nixon's resignation, time to get the nation's problems under control. Meanwhile, many Reagan supporters were urging him to challenge Ford for the Republican nomination in 1976. Had Nixon managed to finish his second term, it was widely thought it would be Reagan's "turn" to be nominated in 1976.

By the summer of 1975, Reagan permitted an exploratory committee to form on his behalf. In November he announced he would be a candidate for the nomination.

The 1976 primary season was closely fought by the Reagan and Ford camps. The delegate count was not certain when the party's convention opened. Ford went on to win the nomination. Reagan made a number of appearances on behalf of the Republican ticket, although Democrat Jimmy Carter managed a narrow victory in the November election.

The 1980 Election

By 1978, support for a Reagan candidacy in 1980 grew in size and strength. By late 1979 he declared his candidacy again. There were several other Republicans in the race at the beginning, but it soon devolved to Reagan and George H. W. Bush. Bush won the Iowa caucuses, but Reagan had an overwhelming victory in the New Hampshire primary.

By the time of the Republican convention in July, the economic and foreign affairs problems of President Carter were driving voters away from the Democrats and toward the Reagan-led Republicans. In November, Reagan defeated Carter by 489 electoral votes to 44.

The Presidency

Ronald Reagan had three main goals as president: straighten out the economy and get it growing again; curb the growth of the federal government and undue regulation; and bring the Cold War to a successful conclusion. He accomplished the first and third and made headway on the second.

In 1981 he successfully engineered the passage of an across-the-board tax-rate reduction for American taxpayers. Despite nearly dying in an attempted assassination in late March, he recovered quickly, addressed a joint session of Congress, and personally lobbied many of its members.

Projections were that the government would lose revenue with the passage of the tax bill. Instead, the new economic activity generated by it resulted in approximately $500 billion in new government revenue. Although in 1981 Reagan faced a recession as a fallout from previous years, by late 1982 the full effect of the tax-rate cut began. From then on well into George H. W. Bush's term, the nation experienced one of the largest, longest periods of economic expansion in its history.

During his campaign Reagan said that, as president, he would spend "whatever it takes" to make sure the United States could not be headed by the Soviet Union in armaments. This was part of what turned out to be his strategy to bring the Cold War to a successful conclusion. His basic plan was to force the Soviets to choose between escalating their arms spending or coming to the bargaining table. He knew that the Kremlin was spending a far larger portion of its budget on arms than was the United States. His strategy played out it various ways, all intended to push the Soviets toward bankruptcy so they would make the decision to come to the negotiating table. In March 1983, for example, he announced the Strategic Defense Initiative, a defensive shield of high-tech weapons to intercept incoming nuclear missiles. The Soviets knew the United States had the technical and monetary resources to make this a reality at some point and they did not.

From the time he and Mikhail Gorbachev first met, at Geneva in 1985, Gorbachev's objective was to get Reagan to put the SDI "on the shelf." When he put this to Reagan at the Reykjavik summit in October 1986, Reagan said no. The Soviets could not continue spending on conventional and nuclear arms and match the SDI without bankrupting themselves. Gorbachev had played his last card, and Reagan had trumped it. There was nothing left but for Gorbachev to bring the Cold War to an end.

As for curbing the growth of the federal government, Reagan was less successful, but he did promote welfare reform (which was passed after he had left office) and did reduce a number of regulations.

In late 1986 the Iran-Contra affair came to light. Knowing how much Reagan wanted to free American hostages held by Hezbollah, some of his administration's officials offered Iran weaponry (in its war with Iraq) as leverage to get Iran to have the hostages released. Separately, other officials took the money from this activity and channeled it to the Contra rebels fighting the Sandinista government in Nicaragua. Congressional Democrats argued that the money transfer was illegal. Reagan named a commission to launch an investigation. Congress held hearings. An independent counsel was appointed. Reagan had been unaware of the details of the affair. When he found them out, he apologized to the nation. Reagan's approval rating dropped steadily during this period, because trust in him had eroded.

As tensions with the USSR lessened and the tide of democracy began to swell across the unfree nations of central and eastern Europe, Reagan's approval ratings rebounded, and when he retired from office in January 1989 he was a popular president.

In Retirement

The first few years of Reagan's retirement were busy. He traveled to Asia and several times to Europe. He was welcomed as a hero in Poland and even in Moscow. At home, he spoke to civic groups and occasionally to party groups. He completed his autobiography, *An American Life*, in 1990. Occasionally he commented on current events in newspaper op-ed articles.

In November 1994 came his moving letter to his fellow Americans announcing that he had been diagnosed with Alzheimer's disease. His travel and speaking schedule had ended after the funeral of Richard Nixon in late April of that year. After his Alzheimer's announcement, he continued to go daily to his office in Los Angeles to greet friends, former associates, and well-wishers. This continued until 1998, when his life became entirely private. He died at home on June 5, 2004.

A state funeral was held at the National Cathedral in Washington, D.C., and a second service that afternoon at the Ronald Reagan Presidential Library in Simi Valley, California, after which he was buried at the site he had chosen overlooking the Pacific Ocean.

In the years since his death, Reagan's accomplishments have become appreciated by ever greater numbers of Americans, while the shortcomings tend to recede into the background. Missed by many is his infectious optimism about the creative ability, willingness to work hard, and the generosity of the American people. He was convinced that these traits made the United States an exceptional country. In his farewell address from the Oval Office, he said, "I've spoken of the shining city all my political life, but I don't know if I ever quite communicated what I saw when I said it. In my mind it was a tall, proud city, built on rocks stronger than oceans, wind-swept, God-blessed and teeming with people of all kinds living in harmony and peace; a city with free ports that hummed with commerce and creativity. And, if there had to be city walls, the walls had doors and the doors were open to anyone with the will and the heart to get there. That's how I saw it and see it still."

Chapter Notes

Chapter One

1. Whiteside County, IL, obituaries, 1900, www.genealogytrails/ill/whiteside (accessed August 2011).

Chapter Two

1. Newspaper clipping, Reagan Archives, Melnick Library, Eureka College, Eureka, IL. Date uncertain.

2. Anne Edwards, *Early Reagan* (New York: William Morrow and Co., 1987), 33–34.

Chapter Three

1. Ronald Reagan, with Richard G. Hubler, *Where's the Rest of Me?* (New York: Elsevier-Dutton Publishing Co., 1965), 11.

2. Ibid., 12

Chapter Four

1. Ronald Reagan, with Richard G. Hubler, *Where's the Rest of Me?* (New York: Elsevier-Dutton Publishing Co., 1965), 13.

2. Anne Edwards, *Early Reagan* (New York: William Morrow and Co., 1987), 40.

Chapter Five

1. Ronald Reagan, with Richard G. Hubler, *Where's the Rest of Me?* (New York: Elsevier-Dutton Publishing Co., 1965), 15.

2. Joan Johnson, "Tampico, Illinois," *Illinois Heritage*: January–February 2011.

3. Ibid.

4. Anne Edwards, *Early Reagan* (New York: William Morrow and Co., 1987), 44.

Chapter Six

1. Anne Edwards, *Early Reagan* (New York: William Morrow and Co., 1987), 51–52.

2. Ronald Reagan, with Richard G. Hubler, *Where's the Rest of Me?* (New York: Elsevier-Dutton Publishing Co., 1965), 18–19.

3. Edwards, *Early Reagan*, 53.

4. Ibid., 57.

5. Reagan, *Where's the Rest of Me?* 9.

6. Lou Cannon, *Governor Reagan: His Rise to Power* (New York: Public Affairs, 2003), 19. In 1984, Reagan, then president, wrote to Jean H. Wright, daughter-in-law of the author, recounting this episode in his life: "After reading it and thinking about it for a few days, I went to my mother and told her I wanted to declare my faith and be baptized."

Chapter Seven

1. Anne Edwards, *Early Reagan* (New York: William Morrow and Co., 1987), 61.

2. Ronald Reagan, with Richard G. Hubler, *Where's the Rest of Me?* (New York: Elsevier-Dutton Publishing Co., 1965), 21.

3. *Dixon Telegraph* / saukvalley.com, "I Never Think of Him as Ronald," June18, 2011.

4. Reagan, *Where's the Rest of Me?* 21.

5. Edwards, *Early Reagan*, 69.

6. Reagan, *Where's the Rest of Me?* 17.

Chapter Eight

1. Ronald Reagan, with Richard G. Hubler, *Where's the Rest of Me?* (New York: Elsevier-Dutton Publishing Co., 1965), 23.

2. Ibid., 26.

3. Anne Edwards, *Early Reagan* (New York: William Morrow and Co., 1987), 95.

4. Ronald Reagan, *An American Life* (New York: Simon & Schuster, 1990), 48.

5. Ibid.

6. Ibid, 21.

7. Edwards, *Early Reagan*, 100, 101.

8. Ibid., 102.

9. Reagan, *An American Life*, 51–52.

10. Interview of Ronald Reagan, by *PM Magazine*, WCIA-TV, Champaign, IL, 1985.

11. *Chicago Sun-Times*, April 30, 1967.

Chapter Nine

1. Ronald Reagan, *An American Life* (New York: Simon & Schuster, 1990), 52.

2. Ibid., 57

3. Lou Cannon, *Governor Reagan: His Rise to Power* (New York: Public Affairs, 2003), 32.

4. *Chicago Sun-Times*, April 23, 1967.

5. Reagan, *An American Life*, 54.

6. *Woodford County (IL) Journal*, May 6, 1982.

Chapter Ten

1. Anne Edwards, *Early Reagan* (New York: William Morrow and Co., 1987), 121–23.

2. Reagan corresponded with Margaret's parents, Ben and Helen Cleaver, for many years. In a May 24, 1973, letter he wrote, "Those were wonderful years in Dixon. I know that time tinges things with gold, and having survived sorrow and troubles they look smaller, but even so, it was a wonderful time."

Appendix A • Visiting Reagan's Illinois

You may be among the many Americans who enjoy visiting presidential sites—birthplaces, boyhood homes, retreats, grave sites. All are places where one can learn about the forty-three men (actually forty-two, if you count Grover Cleveland only once) who have held the office and the forces that shaped them and their presidencies.

In the case of Ronald Reagan, his increasing popularity as a major president has drawn attention to the people and places that helped shape his character. They were and are all in northwestern Illinois. In 1998 a group of citizens formed the Ronald Reagan Trail Association to link the towns in which he lived and often traveled through. On May 21, 1999, the Illinois State General Assembly designated the planned route as the **Ronald Reagan Trail**.

To experience the sites and places of Ronald Reagan's youth, a three-day trip would be ideal to cover the entire 225-mile trail without rushing.

Eureka College is a good place to begin. It is approximately twenty miles east of Peoria on U.S. Highway 24. This is where Reagan graduated with an economics-sociology major in 1932. A walk through the tree-shaded campus is enjoyable, with its mixture of stately Victorian-era brick buildings and contemporary ones. At the Donald B. Cerf Center is the Ronald Reagan Museum, featuring more than two thousand items, most of them donated by the Reagan family, beginning in 1975. Items recall all the periods of his life from childhood through his presidency. Hours: during the school year, Monday–Friday, 8 a.m.–9 p.m.; Saturday, 10 a.m.–6 p.m.; Sunday, noon–9 p.m. During the summer, Monday–Friday, 8 a.m.–4 p.m.; Saturday, 10 a.m.–2 p.m.; closed Sunday and holidays. Admission is free. For information call 309 467-6407.

From Eureka College and the town of Eureka, head west through the town of Washington to Peoria. From there head west on

Interstate 74 approximately fifty miles to **Galesburg**. That is where the Reagan family lived for a little less than two years (1916–17) when young Ronald was in kindergarten and first grade.

From Galesburg go west on U.S. Highway 34 to **Monmouth** (approximately fifteen miles). The Reagans lived here from early 1918 until August 1919, and this is where the young Ronald witnessed the loud and colorful street celebrations of the World War I armistice.

From Monmouth, double back around Galesburg, onto I-74 heading north to I-80, then east on I-80 to State Highway 40. Turn left (north) and proceed approximately eighteen miles to County Highway 12 (Hahnaman Road). Turn left (west) and proceed approximately eight miles to **Tampico,** the town of Reagan's birth.

The Ronald Reagan Birthplace and Museum is at 111 Main Street (tel. 815 622-8705; e-mail: reaganbirthplace@thewisp.net or garyjoan@thewisp.net. Contact: Joan Johnson). Visitors will see the second-story apartment where he was born on February 6, 1911, above what was then a bakery and later a bank (now restored).

From Tampico, take Highway 12 back to State Highway 40. Go left (north) on 40 (eight miles) to I-88, then northeast on I-88 about 17 miles to the junction with State Highway 26, just south of **Dixon**, the small city which the Reagan brothers called their hometown. There is much to see in Dixon:

The Loveland Museum in the Loveland Community House, 513 W. 2nd Street (815 284-2741), has an entire floor devoted to the region's history, with about one-third of it set aside for Reagan exhibits, including a plaque that marked the spot where lifeguard Ronald Reagan cut seventy-seven notches in an old log at Lowell Park beach to commemorate all the lives he saved. There is also a large painting of the work crew he assembled at the Disciples of Christ Church to make the furnace room into a Sunday school classroom. (Phone ahead for times and days of availability.)

The First Christian Church (Disciples of Christ), 123 S. Hennepin Avenue (815 288-1222), where Reagan was baptized, has a Reagan Room with much interesting material. (Telephone for times and days of availability.)

The Dixon Library, 221 S. Hennepin Avenue (815 284-7261) is the place where Ronald Reagan spent many happy hours reading and usually took out two books a week.

Lowell Park is at 2114 Lowell Park Road (815 284-3306), about two miles northeast of the city on the western side of the Rock River. Although there is no longer swimming at the beach, you can see it much as it was in Ronald Reagan's lifeguard days. Also, there is a bike/hiking trail leading from Dixon to the park, 3.5 miles. There are many hiking trails in the park's two hundred acres.

There is also the *Dixon Telegraph* Museum at 113 S. Peoria Avenue (815 284-2224). Hours: Monday–Friday, 8 a.m.–5 p.m.; Saturday, 8 a.m.–noon. The museum includes a section devoted to Reagan as well as one to the newspaper's and the city's history.

Finally, there is a fine bronze equestrian statue of Ronald Reagan on the Rock River waterfront.

To complete the Ronald Reagan Trail, take the dogleg some thirty-six miles west of Dixon to **Fulton**, where Ronald Reagan's parents, Jack and Nelle, were married and where several of their ancestors lived. To get there, go south from Dixon to I-88, take I-88 west nine miles to U.S. Highway 30, then Highway 30 northwest twenty-five miles to the Fulton turnoff and follow the signs.

All along the Ronald Reagan Trail there are many inns, bed-and-breakfasts, and restaurants in rural towns with architecture that evokes an earlier time.

Appendix B • Reagan Chronology at Eureka College

September 1928

14 Pays student fees (cash $51, deferred/notes/scholarships $45)

Source: Roll Book, Feb. 1925–Feb. 1930, p. 55

14 Freshman Week begins

Source: Eureka College Catalogue (hereafter "Catalogue"), vol. 27, no. 1

18 Registration

Source: Catalogue, vol. 27, no. 1

Class schedule

Rhetoric 1 Composition and Themes 3 hrs
English Literature 11 Introduction to Literature 2 hrs
Zoology 1 Invertebrate 4 hrs
History 7 History of Civilization 4 hrs
Rhetoric 29 News Writing 2 hrs
Coaching 5 Elementary Fundamentals ½ hr
Physical Education Football and Basketball ½ hr

19 Pledged TKE (Tau Kappa Epsilon)

Source: *Pegasus*, Sept. 24, 1928, vol. 41, no. 1

20 Recitations begin

Source: Catalogue, vol. 27, no. 1

November 1928

6 Pledged Alpha Epsilon Sigma (Drama Club)

Source: *Pegasus*, Nov. 12, 1928, vol. 41, no. 9

23 Football game against Illinois College—home game ("Dad's Day")

Source: *Pegasus*, Nov. 12, 1928, vol. 41, no. 9

24 Went to the Delta Zeta formal dance

Source: *Pegasus*, Nov. 26, 1928, vol. 41, no. 10

The timeline is based on materials at the Mark R. Shenkman Ronald W. Reagan Research Center and College Archives, Melick Library, Eureka College, Eureka, Illinois. It was prepared by Melick Library director, archivist, and Reagan Museum curator Anthony R. Glass and Eureka College student Lauren Carlsen.

28   Thanksgiving recess begins

> Source: Catalogue, vol. 27, no. 1

December 1928

3   Thanksgiving recess ends

> Source: Catalogue, vol. 27, no. 1

7   Went to a mass meeting in the chapel

> Source: *Pegasus,* n.d.

8   Football team "entertained" by the Phi Omega sorority (no mention of Reagan's name, just that the football team was present)

> Source: *Pegasus*, Dec. 11, 1928, vol. 41, no. 11

21   Christmas recess begins

> Source: Catalogue, vol. 27, no. 1

January 1929

2   Christmas recess ends

> Source: Catalogue, vol. 27, no. 1

28   Midyear examinations begin

> Source: Catalogue, vol. 27, no. 1

February 1929

1   Midyear examinations end

> Source: Catalogue, vol. 27, no. 1

4   Pays student fees ($0 cash, scholarship $45, deferment $45)

> Source: Roll Book, Feb. 1925–Feb. 1930, p. 64

4   Registration

> Source: Catalogue, vol. 27, no. 1

Class schedule

> Rhetoric 2 Composition and Themes 3 hrs
> English Literature 12 Introduction to Literature 2 hrs
> Zoology 2 Vertebrate 4 hrs
> History 8 History of Civilization 4 hrs
> Rhetoric 30 News Editing and Feature Writing 2 hrs
> Coaching 6 Elementary Fundamentals ½ hr
> Physical Education Football and Basketball ½ hr

5   Recitations begin
   Source: Catalogue, vol. 27, no. 1
6   Founders Day
   Source: Catalogue, vol. 27, no. 1
26   *Pegasus* publishes article about Reagan's debut as a cheerleader
   Source: *Pegasus*, Feb. 26, 1929, vol. 41, no. 19

April 1929

10   Spring recess begins
   Source: Catalogue, vol. 27, no. 1
15   Spring recess ends
   Source: Catalogue, vol. 27, no. 1

May 1929

2   Visited Carlock High School to give readings
   Source: *Pegasus*, May 7, 1929, vol. 41, no. 28

June 1929

4   Final examinations begin
   Source: Catalogue, vol. 27, no. 1
10   Final examinations end
   Source: Catalogue, vol. 27, no. 1
11   66th annual commencement
   Source: Catalogue, vol. 27, no. 1

September 1929

17   Registration
   Source: Catalogue, vol. 28, no. 1
   Class schedule
      English 31 American Literature 2 hrs
      History 23 History of the United States 3 hrs
      French 1 Elementary French
      Public Speaking 33 Oral Interpretation of Literature 2 hrs
      English 45 English Romantic Movement 3 hrs
      Education 21 General Psychology 3 hrs
      Coaching 31 Theory of Training 1/2 hr
      Physical Education 1/2 hr

18 Pays student fees ($45 cash, deferred/notes/scholarship $45)
(was with brother, Neil Reagan)

> Source: Roll Book, Feb. 1925–Feb. 1930, p. 71

19 Recitations begin

> Source: Catalogue, vol. 28, no. 1

October 1929

26 *Pegasus* announces that Reagan will help to write articles for
the *Prism*

> Source: *Pegasus*, Oct. 26, 1929, vol. 42, no. 6

November 1929

2 *Pegasus* mentions Reagan in football lineup—listed as "R.G."
(right guard)

> Source: *Pegasus*, Nov. 2, 1929, vol. 42, no. 7

15 Acted in *The Dover Road* (Margaret Cleaver and Neil Reagan
were also in the cast)

> Source: *Pegasus*, Oct. 26, 1929, vol. 42, no. 6

27 Thanksgiving recess begins

> Source: Catalogue, vol. 28, no. 1

December 1929

1 Thanksgiving recess ends

> Source: Catalogue, vol. 28, no. 1

20 Christmas recess begins

> Source: Catalogue, vol. 28, no. 1

January 1930

6 Christmas recess ends

> Source: Catalogue, vol. 28, no. 1

27 Midyear examinations begin

> Source: Catalogue, vol. 28, no. 1

February 1930

1 Midyear examinations end

> Source: Catalogue, vol. 28, no. 1

3 Pays student fees (cash $0, deferred $45, scholarships $45)

> Source: Roll Book, Feb. 1930–Dec. 1933, p. 1

3   Registration

> Source: Catalogue, vol. 28, no. 1

Class schedule

> English 32 American Literature 2 hrs
> History 24 History of the United States 3 hrs
> French 2 Elementary French
> Coaching 32 Theory of Training ½ hr
> Economics 22 Principles of Economics 3 hrs
> Education 24 Educational Psychology 3 hrs
> Physical Education ½ hr

8   Wrote a letter to *Pegasus* about Eureka College spirit

> Source: *Pegasus*, Feb. 8, 1930, vol. 42, no. 17

8   Was a guest at the Phi Omega Valentine's dance (other guests included Margaret Cleaver and Neil Reagan)

> Source: *Pegasus*, Feb. 15, 1930, vol. 42, no. 18

9   Was presented a football sweater (also known as the Eureka E sweater; was presented to him by Coach McKinzie)

> Source: *Pegasus*, Feb. 15, 1930, vol. 42, no. 18

13   Was nominated for president of the booster club

> Source: *Pegasus*, Feb. 15, 1930, vol. 42, no. 18

15   Was elected Pylortes for TKE

> Source: *Pegasus*, Feb. 15, 1930, vol. 42, no. 18

April 1930

2–7   Spring recess

> Source: Catalogue, vol. 28, no. 1

19   Received honorable mention for excellence in individual acting at Northwestern University (no specific date given; Alpha Epsilon Sigma won $25 for its adaption of *Aria da Capo*)

> Source: *Pegasus*, Apr. 19, 1930, vol. 42, no. 26

26   Wrote a letter to *Pegasus* about fraternity offices being counted in the point system

> Source: *Pegasus*, Apr. 26, 1930, vol. 42, no. 27

June 1930

2–7 Final examinations

Source: Catalogue, vol. 28, no. 1

10 70th annual commencement

Source: Catalogue, vol. 28, no. 1

September 1930

17 Pays student fees (cash $45, scholarships $45)

Source: Roll Book, Feb. 1930–Dec. 1933, p. 11

17 Registration

Source: Catalogue, vol. 29, no. 1

Class schedule

History 29 English History to 1689 2 hrs
French 3 Intermediate French 4 hrs
Bible 3 Life of Christ 3 hrs
Economics 21 Principles of Economics 3 hrs
Sociology 43 Principles of Sociology 3 hrs
Physical Education Footbal ½ hr

18 Recitations begin

Source: Catalogue, vol. 29, no. 1

October 1930

10 Football game against Macomb—away game

Source: *Pegasus*, Oct. 11, 1930, vol. 43, no. 2

18 Football game against Elmhurst—first game on newly dedicated McKinzie Field—home game

Source: *Pegasus*, Oct. 16, 1930, vol. 43, no. 3

24 Formally opened homecoming as Booster Club president (took place in front of the chapel; brother Neil helped to open)

Source: *Pegasus*, Oct. 23, 1930, vol. 43, no. 4

25 Football game against Normal—home game

Source: *Pegasus*, Oct. 16, 1930, vol. 43, no. 3

25 Presented prizes to teams and individuals for different acts and events at the stunt show

Source: *Pegasus*, Oct. 23, 1930, vol. 43, no. 4

November 1930

1   Football game against Wesleyan—away game
>Source: *Pegasus*, Oct. 16, 1930, vol. 43, no. 3

8   Football game against Carthage—home game
>Source: *Pegasus*, Oct. 16, 1930, vol. 43, no. 3

15   Football game against Mt. Morris—away game
>Source: *Pegasus*, Oct. 16, 1930, vol. 43, no. 3

22   Football game against Illinois College—home game
>Source: *Pegasus*, Oct. 16, 1930, vol. 43, no. 3

26   Thanksgiving recess begins
>Source: Catalogue, vol. 29, no. 1

December 1930

1   Thanksgiving recess ends
>Source: Catalogue, vol. 29, no. 1

18   Was quoted in *Pegasus*
>Source: *Pegasus*, Dec. 18, 1930, vol. 43, no. 11

20   Christmas recess begins
>Source: Catalogue, vol. 29, no. 1

January 1931

5   Christmas recess ends
>Source: Catalogue, vol. 29, no. 1

26–31 Midyear examinations
>Source: Catalogue, vol. 29, no. 1

February 1931

2   Pays student fees (cash $0, deferred $45, scholarship $45)
>Source: Roll Book, Feb. 1930–Dec. 1933, p. 18

2   Registration
>Source: Catalogue, vol. 29, no. 1

Class schedule

History 30 English History since 1689 2 hrs
French 4 Intermediate French 4 hrs
Bible 4 Apostolic Age 3 hrs
Rhetoric 28 Advanced Composition 2hrs

> Economics 24 Immigration 3hrs
> History 40 Europe since 1815 3hrs
> Physical Education Football ½ hr

3   Recitations begin

> Source: Catalogue, vol. 29, no. 1

6   Founders Day

> Source: Catalogue, vol. 29, no. 1

March 1931

14   Attended the Delta Zeta St. Patrick's Day function (Margaret Cleaver was also in attendance)

> Source: *Pegasus*, Mar. 19, 1931, vol. 43, no. 20

22   Led a discussion about world peace and the chances of another war

> Source: *Pegasus*, Mar. 19, 1931, vol. 43, no. 20

April 1931

1–6 Spring recess

> Source: Catalogue, vol. 29, no. 1

May 1931

7   Published a letter in *Pegasus* addressed to visitors

> Source: *Pegasus*, May 7, 1931, vol. 43, no. 25

June 1931

1–6 Final examinations

> Source: Catalogue, vol. 29, no. 1

9   71st annual commencement

> Source: Catalogue, vol. 29, no. 1

September 1931

16   Registration

> Source: Catalogue, vol. 30, no. 1

Class schedule

> Economics 53 Money and Banking 4 hrs
> Economics 56 Insurance 2 hrs
> Sociology 27 Social Problems 3 hrs

Economics 59 Senior Economics 4 hrs
Public Speaking 3 Fundamentals of Speech 1½ hrs
Philosophy 53 Reflective Living 3 hrs
Physical Education Football ½ hr

17 Pays student fees (cash $0, deferred $45, scholarships $45)

Source: Roll Book, Feb. 1930–Dec. 1933, p. 29

17 Recitations begin

Source: Catalogue, vol. 30, no. 1

21 Jack Reagan visits Ronald and Neil at TKE House

Source: *Pegasus*, Sept. 24, 1931, vol. 44, no. 1

October 1931

19 Celebrated engagement to Margaret Cleaver at the Delta Zeta house with five pounds of Fannie May's

Source: *Pegasus*, Oct. 22, 1931, vol. 44, no. 5

30 Acted in *Imaginary Invalid* (Margaret Cleaver also acted in this play)

Source: *Pegasus*, Nov. 5, 1931, vol. 44, no. 7

November 1931

18 Called the Eureka College Senate to order

Source: *Pegasus*, Nov. 25, 1931, vol. 44, no. 8

21 Was "entertained" by the TKE pledges (Margaret Cleaver also in attendance)

Source: *Pegasus*, Nov. 25, 1931, vol. 44, no. 8

25–30 Thanksgiving recess

Source: Catalogue, vol. 30, no. 1

December 1931

10 Article published in *Pegasus* about Reagan being a lifeguard (article claimed he saved sixty-some lives that summer and also called him a dentist for saving a man's dentures)

Source: *Pegasus*, Dec. 10, 1931, vol. 44, no. 10

22 Christmas recess begins

Source: Catalogue, vol. 30, no. 1

January 1932

4 Christmas recess ends

Source: Catalogue, vol. 30, no. 1

25–31 Midyear examinations

Source: Catalogue, vol. 30, no. 1

February 1932

1–3 Pays student fees ($17 cash, $45 scholarship, $28 deferred) (Roll books do not say which day it was, just that he paid sometime between Feb. 1 and Feb. 3)

Source: Roll Book, Feb. 1930–Dec. 1933, p. 35

1 Registration

Source: Catalogue, vol. 30, no. 1

Class schedule

Economics 60 Senior Economics 4 hrs

Rhetoric 28 Creative Writing 2 hrs

Sociology 46 Criminology 3 hrs

Economics 58 Investments 2 hrs

Education 49 Principles of Education 3 hrs

Economics 25 Labor Problems 3 hrs

Physical Education Football ½ hr

2 Recitations begin

Source: Catalogue, vol. 30, no. 1

6 Founder's Day

Source: Catalogue, vol. 30, no. 1

March 1932

23–28 Spring recess

Source: Catalogue, vol. 30, no. 1

April 1932

1 Comic was printed in *Pegasus* about Reagan (an April Fool's joke)

Source: *Pegasus*, Apr. 1, 1932, vol. 44, no. 22

May 1932

5   Played for TKE Fraternity in the "Kitty" ball league
       Source: *Pegasus*, May 12, 1932, vol. 44

12   Senior biography is published in *Pegasus*
       Source: *Pegasus*, May 12, 1932, vol. 44

30   Final examinations begin
       Source: Catalogue, vol. 30, no. 1

June 1932

4   Final examinations end
       Source: Catalogue, vol. 30, no. 1

5   Baccalaureate sermon
       Source: Catalogue, vol. 31, no. 1

6   Pays last student fees (for graduation)
       Source: Roll Book, Feb. 1930–Dec. 1933, p. 40

6   Acted in *Taming of the Shrew* (Margaret Cleaver also acted)
       Source: *Pegasus*, May 12, 1932, vol. 44

7   72nd annual commencement
       Source: Catalogue, vol. 30, no. 1

7   Planting of the Ivy
       Source: Catalogue, vol. 31, no. 1

145

Appendix C • Going Home: Reagan's Later Visits

On February 7, 2011, after being a panelist at a Reagan Centennial Year conference at Eureka College ("Reagan and the Midwest"), Fred Barnes, executive editor of the *Weekly Standard*, wrote in that magazine, "The more we learn about him, the more we realize his values, his outlook on life, his embrace of leadership, his political styles and, to a significant extent, his political ideology were shaped by the first 26 years of his life in Illinois hamlets such as Dixon, Tampico and Eureka. Reagan was, first and foremost, a small-town Midwesterner at heart."

Over the years following his move to Southern California, Reagan's rural Illinois pulled him back time and again. He first returned to the town of his birth, Tampico, in 1950 when he and his mother, Nelle, were grand marshals of the town's annual homecoming parade in July.

On Monday, February 23, 1976, he led the national press covering his presidential campaign on a tour of his second-floor apartment birthplace. This was followed by a reunion with his third-grade classmates.

On Mother's Day, 1992, he and wife, Nancy, accompanied by biographer Edmund Morris, arrived in Tampico, first attending services at the Disciples of Christ church. After that they visited his birthplace, by then preserved as a museum, and later had lunch at the Dutch Diner.

Back in 1955, Morrison, another town that figured in his boyhood (an aunt, uncle, and cousins lived on a farm there), was a stop on one of his General Electric plant tours. It is about twenty miles from Tampico. He visited it on October 17 and 18. He toured the GE Appliance Control plant there, met the workers, gave a talk, visited the local high school (where Enos "Bud" Cole, a college classmate and fraternity brother was principal), and visited with both a first and second cousin (the latter, Gene M. Smith, worked at the GE plant).

Dixon, the small city he considered his hometown, received more visits, and Eureka College, his alma mater, received still more.

Going Home to Dixon

After moving to California in the spring of 1937, he returned to Dixon eight times.

In September 1941 he arrived by train with Dixon native Louella Parsons, then Hollywood's leading columnist, for "Louella Parsons Day." His film *International Squadron* had its premier at the Dixon Theater. Stars accompanying them were Bob Hope, his sidekick Jerry Colonna, George Montgomery, Ann Rutherford, Joe E. Brown, and husband-and-wife team Ben Lyon and Bebe Daniels.

During August 20–24, 1950, Ronald and his mother, Nelle, took part in "Injun Summer Days," during which he dedicated the city's Memorial Pool, the Reynolds Field softball diamond, and a new wing at the KSB Hospital. He rode friend Jean Rorer's palomino in the One Thousand Trail Riders' Parade. One evening he addressed a dinner audience of four hundred at the Masonic Temple. They stayed at Hazelwood, the estate of Charles Walgreen's widow, Myrtle. Nelle stayed on for three weeks to visit old friends.

On April 20, 1963, he spoke at the Dixon High School honors banquet.

Almost thirteen years later, on the same day he visited Tampico on his campaign tour, February 23, 1976, he took his bus and entourage to see Dixon, his boyhood home, and Lowell Park, and speak at a rally in his honor at the Dixon High School gymnasium.

In August 1978 he attended the school's all-classes reunion.

In fall 1980, during his presidential campaign, he paid another visit to Dixon, speaking at a rally for him at the high school.

On February 6, 1984, when was he president, he and brother Neil visited their boyhood home on South Hennepin Avenue. Nancy Reagan was with them.

Twelve years later, after a "sentimental journey" back to his birthplace in Tampico, on Mother's Day 1992, he, Nancy, and biographer Edmund Morris drove about Dixon to see some of the sites of his youth.

Returning to Eureka College

At his commencement address on May 9, 1982, Ronald Reagan succinctly stated the importance of Eureka College to him when he said, "Everything that has been good in my life began here."

Between 1934 and 1999 he returned fourteen times to the campus for visits. He also served as a member of the college's board of trustees for three six-year terms.

His first return to Eureka was only two years after his graduation. In 1934 he participated in a convocation on campus about radio broadcasting. By 1941 he was a famous movie actor and returned during the trip that included a visit to Dixon. In 1947 he returned to crown the Pumpkin Queen.

In 1955 he attended Eureka's homecoming festivities celebrating the one hundredth anniversary of the school's charter. On June 9, 1957, he was the commencement speaker and received an honorary doctor of humane letters degree.

Accompanied by wife Nancy, he made a brief campus visit on Saturday, January 21, 1961. The Reagans had lunch with the college's president and several faculty members and students, and he made brief remarks.

On April 1, 1967, he was the main speaker at the dedication of the college's Melick Library. In 1970 he was back again, along with his brother Neil, for the dedication of the Reagan Physical Education Center, named after them.

He was back on campus February 5–6, 1977, to speak at the kick-off rally for the Eureka College Eighties Fund campaign, of which he was honorary chairman. In 1979 he was the speaker at the Honors Day Banquet on campus and was named chairman of the college's National Advisory Council. In October 1980 he visited the campus for a pep rally during his presidential campaign.

On May 9, 1982, his commencement address was a major one of his presidency, in which he called for the beginning of Strategic Arms Reductions Talks (START) with the Soviet Union.

Not quite two years later, on February 7, 1984, he attended the 129th anniversary of the college's founding as the first in the Time Distinguished Speaker series. In his talk, he reaffirmed his determination to reach agreements with Moscow on reducing the size of the superpowers' nuclear arsenals.

Twice during the Reagan presidency, Eureka College went to Washington. In 1986 the president was the honored guest at a benefit dinner at the Willard Hotel for Eureka's Ronald Reagan Leadership Program. The next year, the president was the host in the White House for Eureka's Ronald Reagan Fellows and leading supporters of the college.

In 1992, retired from the White House, Reagan gave his third and final Eureka commencement speech on the sixtieth anniversary of his own graduation.

Dutch Reagan as His Friends Remembered Him

Dixon

"The values he has now were the things Nelle taught him in the home. If things go wrong, then something good will happen. All his life he believed this."

—Helen Lawton, next-door neighbor in high school days,
in *Heartland* magazine, 1992

"While he was a great communicator even in school, I don't think any of us had the vaguest idea he would become our president."

—Jean Rorer, classmate who appeared with him in two plays at Dixon High School in 1926–27

Eureka College

"I started as a bookkeeper the same day Ronald Reagan started as a student. He was poor and worked his way through school by washing dishes, raking and mowing—things like that. He was such a favorite of all the young people in town. And he was always fair and honest. He wouldn't stand for cheating in athletics."

—Irene Reynolds, *Chicago American*, September 24, 1967

"We talked about politics then, but it never entered anybody's head that Dutch would go into politics. He had a lot of ideas."

—Enos "Bud" Cole, classmate and fraternity brother, *Chicago Sun-Times*, April 30, 1967

"He was a fellow you couldn't help but like. Active in everything."

—Clinton Melnick, a major benefactor of the college, *Chicago American*, September 24, 1967

"He's a genuinely nice and honest person."

—Edith Fraiser Taflan, a fellow student at Eureka, *Monticello (IL) Journal-Republican*, August 7, 1980

"He was one of the few people I know who is really what he seems to be. Reagan has that rare quality of loyalty to his friends and college. His love for Eureka is not cultivated sentimentality—it really exists."

—Ira Langston, president of Eureka College, *Chicago Sun-Times*, April 30, 1967

Bibliography

Cannon, Lou. *Governor Reagan: His Rise to Power*. New York: Public Affairs, 2003.

Edwards, Anne. *Early Reagan*. New York: William Morrow and Co., 1987.

First Christian Church (Disciples of Christ), Dixon, Illinois. "The Reagan Family and the First Christian Church," no date.

Hannaford, Peter, and Charles Hobbs. *Remembering Reagan*. Washington, DC: Regnery Publishing, 1994.

Holmes, Raymond. *An Autobiography*. Richmond, VA: Privately published, 1998.

Johnson, Joan. "Tampico, Illinois," *Illinois Heritage*, January–February 2011.

Reagan, Ronald. *An American Life*. New York: Simon & Schuster, 1990.

Reagan, Ronald, with Richard G. Hubler. *Where's the Rest of Me?* New York: Elsevier-Dutton Publishing Co., 1965.